A LIVING LETTER
FOR THE
CHILDREN'S HOUR

A LIVING LETTER FOR THE CHILDREN'S HOUR

by KENNETH N. TAYLOR

Illustrated by ROBERT G. DOARES

MOODY PRESS • CHICAGO

Library of Congress Catalog Card Number: 68-26407

Revised Edition

31 32 Printing/LC/Year 87 86 85

ISBN 0-8024-0062-0

Contents

Introduction

THE REASON FOR THIS BOOK is that Christian children and young people need the mighty truths of the Pauline Epistles. These great New Testament letters have transformed the church through the ages and radically changed millions of Christians. Moreover, children need these truths in early years, not only after they have grown up.

But all too often the New Testament letters are largely cut off from children (and older readers of the Bible too) by the bigness of Paul's thoughts expressed in few words. Often he uses technical expressions with a world of meaning for the mature, instructed Christian, but far from clear to others until explained.

Can other words be used to make his meaning clearer? Yes, but sometimes it takes several words or even a sentence to make a single word meaningful. When Paul says, for instance, "Moreover the law entered" (Romans 5:20) this can be expanded to read, "Later on, God gave the Ten Commandments." But this change makes use of the word *God* not found in the original text. And, for the sake of getting across the idea

7

in words more easily understood, it uses "Ten Commandments" instead of "the law."

Is this an exact translation? No, it is called a paraphrase or adaptation. It is an attempt to give Paul's meaning as exactly as possible to a new reader of the Scriptures. You see, Paul wrote 2,000 years ago in Greek, a language far different from the English which you and I speak. Therefore the purpose of this adaptation is to present Paul's message in words that he himself would use if he were writing for you and me today.

In doing so, good objections can easily be raised. For instance, in the example, "the law" may mean more than the Ten Commandments: the Old Testament system of sacrifices may also be in Paul's mind. But if "The Ten Commandments" approximately represents to the reader the idea Paul had in mind, then it seems legitimate to use it, believing that the inexperienced Bible reader will get much more of God's message from this approximately correct phrase which he understands than from the words "the law" which mean something quite different than he thinks.

Such adaptations, by the way, are not new. More than a hundred years ago Locke produced his paraphrase of the book of Romans, and in the last few years there have been many New Testament paraphrases. Each of these serves a good purpose and it is hoped that this book will find the Lord's blessing for families in their family devotional period.

1
The Strange Adventure of Paul

Young Paul and his police force were on the way to Damascus to arrest every Christian they could find and bring them in chains to Jerusalem for trial and severe punishment. Paul hated Christians with all his heart and believed that he was pleasing God when he hurt them, because these Christians believed that the way to heaven was through Jesus Christ instead of by obeying the Jewish laws. This made the Jews, including Paul, furiously angry; they felt that to talk about Christ as Saviour was an insult. They thought Jesus was a wicked deceiver who had led people away from the truths of God. Paul, as a young Jewish leader, felt very strongly about it and that is why he was going so angrily to Damascus that day; he was anxious to hunt down every Christian in town and to stamp out Christianity forever.

9

Then God took a hand in the matter; for suddenly a great light shone down from heaven upon Paul as he walked along the road, and a voice spoke to him. It was the voice of God. "Saul," God said, "why are you trying to hurt me?" (Saul was Paul's other name before he became a Christian.)

Paul, as you might guess, was trembling so hard that he fell down, but gasped out a question, "Sir, who are you?"

And the Lord said, "I am Jesus—the One you are persecuting."

Then Paul, lying there trembling and completely overcome, said, "Lord, what do you want me to do?"

And the Lord said, "Get up and go on into Damascus and there you will be shown what to do next."

The men who were with Paul heard the voice but didn't see anyone. They were speechless with surprise and fear as they helped Paul stand up again. But Paul was now completely blind, so they had to lead him along into the city. He stayed blind for the next three days and during that time he neither ate nor drank.

Then the Lord sent one of His men, Ananias, who lived in Damascus, to Paul. "Go over to Straight Street," the Lord told Ananias, "and ask for the house where Judas lives and there you will find Saul of Tarsus praying." (Remember, Saul was Paul's other name.)

Ananias went, but he was scared. He'd heard of Paul, as every Christian had, and knew he had come to Damascus to arrest and hurt all of them.

But the Lord said, "Don't worry about it, Ananias. I have chosen Paul to carry the gospel to the Gentiles and to kings. And, oh, what terrible things he is going to suffer for the sake of My name."

So Ananias found Paul and put his hands on him and suddenly Paul could see again! He was baptized and immediately began to preach to the Jews, telling them that Christ is the risen Son of God.

And, of course, then all the forces of Satan broke loose against Paul. The Jews tried to kill him and the only way he could escape was by the Christians putting him in a basket and using ropes to lower him over the side of the city wall.

Paul got back to Jerusalem safely and tried to join the Christians but they were naturally afraid of him until Barnabas, one of the well-known Christians, took him with him to one of the secret meetings of the Christians and explained how the Lord had met Paul there on the road, and now Paul was a Christian too. Immediately he began to preach boldly in Jerusalem but again the Jews set about to quiet him by killing him, so Paul was sent off to the city of Tarsus, his hometown; and the church of Jerusalem had peace for awhile because Paul, their former great enemy, had deserted his job of persecuting them and had become their friend!

Paul became the greatest missionary and leader of the church of those days, spending his life going from city to city to preach the good news concerning Christ to the Jews who would listen, and especially to the Gentiles, for they had never before heard of the love of God for them.

It was a long, lonely, terribly hard life—full of imprisonment in chains, many beatings, whippings and once he was even stoned and left for dead. Yet they were happy days, too, for God used Paul mightily everywhere he went and many little churches were started, and they in turn started others. So by the time Paul was an old man, thousands upon thousands of people had heard the gospel from his lips and had believed and God had given them eternal life.

Meanwhile, Paul had kept up a steady correspondence with the churches of various cities, instructing, encouraging, scolding and rejoicing with them—helping them in every way he could with his God-given advice. A few of these letters were kept for us and have become parts of the Bible.

It is his great letter to the church in Rome that we will begin to read together tomorrow. This letter has changed millions of lives because, although Paul wrote it, it is really a letter from God Himself to you and me. Perhaps it will change your life too, just as it has changed mine.

SOME QUESTIONS TO ANSWER:
1. Why was Paul going to Damascus?
2. What happened on the way?
3. How did Paul get over being blind?
4. How did he spend the rest of his life?
5. What happened to the letters he wrote?

A PRAYER

Dear Lord, thank You for Jesus and His mighty power. Thank You for showing yourself to Paul there on the road to Damascus and for making him understand that Jesus is the Son of God who died to save us. Thank You that Paul went everywhere preaching the gospel even though he had to go to jail and be beaten for it; and thank You that he wrote the letters in the Bible that help us so much. In Jesus' name. Amen.

2
A Wonderful Letter

JIM BARTON was a student studying physics at the University of Chicago. His teacher was a Christian but Jim wasn't. One day they got to talking about life and its problems and Jim's teacher told him, "There's a letter you ought to read that has answered a lot of people's questions; it's Paul's letter to the people in Rome. I'll get you a copy if you'd like."

So the teacher got a copy of the book of Romans in the Bible and gave it to Jim to read; and he read it with interest and, sure enough, his questions were answered. One night after reading from the letter, Jim couldn't get to sleep. He kept thinking about what the letter said, about God's great kindness to sinful men and how God sent Jesus into the world to save them from their sins. Jim got out of bed and down on his knees and asked God to forgive his sins and to be his Saviour,

and God did as Jim asked; so that night Jim received God'
great gift—eternal life in heaven.

His whole life was changed by reading this letter of Paul'.
that we are going to read together. And I could tell you other
stories, true as this one is, of many others who have read thi
letter and whose lives have been changed as a result, so that
they have become strong men and women of God. Perhaps
your life too will be different as we read it together now. So—
let's begin:

ROMANS 1:1-7

Dear Boys and Girls, Fathers and Mothers there in Rome:
    [1] This letter is from Paul, your old missionary friend and
a slave. Yes, I am a slave of Jesus Christ, and the job He has
given me is to tell everyone everywhere that Jesus has come
to save them.
    [2] Long ago God said He would send His Son, Jesus, into
the world, and these promises were written down in the
Bible.
    [3] He came as a human baby, born into King David's royal
family line.
    [4] But He was also the Son of God by nature. We know this
because when He died, He, amazingly, came back to life again
as Jesus Christ our Lord.
    [5] Jesus has brought to us all of God's kindnesses, and now
He has sent us out everywhere, all around the world, to tell
people what great things God has done for them, so that they
will love Him and obey Him.
    [6] And you dear friends in Rome are among those He loved
so much and He has invited you to be His very own. [7] May all
of the Lord's blessings be yours, and peace from God our
Father and from Jesus Christ our Lord.

SOME QUESTIONS TO ANSWER:

1. Who wrote this letter we have begun to read?
   To whom was the letter sent?

2. Why did Paul say that he was a slave?

   What did Paul feel that his big job in life was?

   What is your job that God has given to you?

A PRAYER

O God, our heavenly Father, thank You for Jesus, Your Son, who came down from heaven to save us. Thank You that we know Him. Help us to tell others about Him and how much He loves them. Please make Your church grow and be strong everywhere, all around the world, and may thousands of people hear and be saved today. In Jesus' name. Amen.

3

Paul Wants to Visit His Friends

THE BIBLE is like dynamite! When you read it to people, wonderful things often happen to them. For instance, there was a robber out in India, leader of a band of murderers. The police were afraid of them and stayed as far away as they could. This robber chieftain boasted that no one would ever catch him alive. He always carried two guns—one to use on other people, and one to use on himself if he ever got caught.

One day he robbed and killed a man who had a Bible in his pocket. The pages in the Bible were good for making cigarettes, by rolling up tobacco in them. So the robber kept the Bible and tore out some pages whenever he needed them.

A few days later, when the robber chief was tearing out a page, he noticed some of the words and saw that there was an interesting story on the little sheet he held there in his hand.

It told about somebody named Jesus who was dying on a cross for other people's sins. The robber sat down and read on and on. Finally he put the torn page back into the Bible so he could read it again. He couldn't forget what he had read, and all day long he kept thinking about it. That night he took out what was left of the Bible and began to read it some more.

And then what happened? God came right into that robber's heart and completely changed it. The robber finally realized how wicked he was. But he learned something else too, that God loved him and had died to take away his sins. So he decided that night to let God control his life. He threw away both his guns and went to the police and let them put him in jail. And he is still there, but he is happy because God is there with him.

Yes, the gospel is God's dynamite to transform lives. That is what Paul tells us in this part of his letter that we are going to read now.

1:8-17

8 Let me say first of all that everywhere I go, people are talking about you! They keep telling me how much you people there in Rome love God and trust Him. How I thank God, through Jesus Christ our Lord, for your testimony and for each one of you.

9 And God knows how often I pray for you. Day and night I talk to Him whom I serve so faithfully in giving out His message concerning His Son, asking Him to help you. 10 One thing I keep praying about is for God to please let me come and see you! 11 I'd give almost anything if I could, because I want to help you know God even better than you do now.

12 And I want you to help me too. I want to share my faith with you and to get some of yours. That way, each of us will help the other.

13 I want you to know this, that I have tried many times to

come to visit you, but it has never worked out. Each time God has sent me somewhere else instead. But now at last I'm able to come and help you just as I have so many of the other churches. [14] For my job is to help everyone, no matter who they are or what they are like. [15] That is why I am so anxious to come to Rome and preach the good news to you too.

[16] I am not embarrassed when it comes to telling people the good news that Christ saves. This good news is the mighty energy that brings to heaven all who trust in Him. God offered this salvation first of all to the Jews, but now He invites everyone to come. [17] This good news that Christ died for us is God's way of saving those who trust in Him. For, as the Bible says in another place, "The person who is made good by trusting God shall live forever."

SOME QUESTIONS TO ANSWER:

1. What is the wonderful message from God that can change a person's whole life? Why is it like dynamite?

2. Where is this message from God written down? Was Paul the first one who knew about it?

3. Why did Paul want to visit Rome? How much did he want to do this?

4. If you had a secret weapon that would blast people into heaven, would you be embarrassed to tell them about it? How would you feel about introducing people to a Friend of yours who could save them from hell and take them to heaven? Why do we sometimes feel so strange about telling others this good news?

A PRAYER

Our Father in heaven, thank You for letting us hear that You died for us. Thank You that we have believed You. Thank You that this good news can change our lives, just as it did the robber chieftain's. Help us to love You and live for You. In Jesus' name we ask these things. Amen.

4
God
Is
Angry

THIS IS NOT A HAPPY STORY but a true one. It is about a boy whose father and mother loved Jesus but for some reason their son didn't seem to understand that he, too, needed a Saviour. He believed in God and tried to be good, but he wasn't a Christian.

Everything seemed to go along all right for several years and the boy grew up and went away to school. The teachers at this school told him that he was foolish to believe in God. They said that there wasn't any God, and he began to believe them.

Then after awhile he thought, well, if there isn't a God then I can do whatever I want to, even things that are wrong, because God won't see me and punish me—since there is no God; and before very long this boy began to swear and steal.

19

Things went from bad to worse and one day when he had been drinking too much, he had a fight with a friend and killed him. The judge said that he must be hanged, and a few weeks later that is the terrible way that he died.

When this boy put God out of his life, sin and death came in. Today in his letter Paul shows us how often this happens, and how entire civilizations have fallen apart in sin because they have turned against God. It is a solemn warning to us here in our country, and to each of us as individuals. Do you have a real Saviour, or is Jesus only a nice person you have heard about? What a difference it makes!

1:18-32

[18] God in heaven is very angry with those who hate Him and who sneer at what He tells them to do. They know better, of course, but they just don't care. [19] They know in their hearts that there is a God, for God made them in such a way that they all know this. [20] For they can see the earth and sky God made, and know at once how great and powerful He is. So they will have no excuse for saying they didn't know there is a God.

[21] They knew about Him all right, but they didn't want Him around. They weren't even thankful for all the kind things He did for them every day. And after awhile they began to think up silly ideas as to what God was like and what He wanted them to do, and the result was that their black hearts became even darker. [22] They went around telling everyone that they were very wise and knew all about God, but instead they became fools. [23] Some of them even took wood that rots and made idols that looked like birds and animals and snakes and men, and said that these things were our glorious, eternal God.

[24] And so God gave up on them and decided to let them do all the bad things they wanted to, no matter how terrible, and to let them do vile, wicked things with each other's

20

bodies. ²⁵ They told lies to themselves about God and said it was all right to pray to the mountains and trees, and to other things God made, but they wouldn't pray to the blessed God who made these things.

²⁶ So God let them go ahead and do wicked things to each other. Women married each other instead of marrying men, even though they knew this was very wrong. ²⁷ And men eagerly married each other instead of marrying women. This is a terrible thing and as a result they became wretchedly unhappy.

²⁸ And so, since they gave up God, and didn't want Him around, God gave them up and let them go ahead and do all the things He didn't want them to, so that they became worse and worse and worse. ²⁹ They are filled up with every kind of sin and wickedness. Here are some of the things they do:

They are never satisfied with what God has given them but want other people's things too.

They keep trying to find something wrong with other people.

They are full of envy and angry because other people have things they don't.

They hate other people, and want to kill them.

They are always ready to argue and fight.

They are sneaky.

They are always whispering about other people and saying evil things behind their backs.

³⁰ They hate God.

They always try to get even with other people.

They are proud and conceited.

They are always boasting about how great they are.

They are always thinking up new ways of sinning.

They won't obey their parents.

³¹ They try to misunderstand.

They break their promises.

They don't love their own families.

They won't accept an apology if someone is sorry about something he has done to them.

They have no mercy, and are always ready to kick a person when he is down and can't help himself.

³² They know these things are wrong, and in the back of their minds they know that God will destroy them for doing all these bad things, and yet they go right ahead and do them and then try to get others to do them too.

SOME QUESTIONS TO ANSWER:

1. Do people know there is a God even without anyone telling them? How do they know?
2. If you see a watch, do you need anyone to tell you that someone made it? Why not?
3. When people see the world and the stars, what can they learn from them about God?
4. What could you say to a person who says he doesn't think there is a God?
5. People who want to sin usually decide that God doesn't care very much. How does this idea compare with the truth they really know deep down in their hearts?

A PRAYER

O God, our heavenly Father, we know that You are great, and that You are terrible in Your anger against sin. Help us not to sin, but to let Jesus live His pure life in us so that we can please You all the time. And help us to pray for those who are living in sin that they might know that God is angry with them and that He loves them still. These things we ask in Jesus' name. Amen.

5
They Thought They Were God's Pets

"HEY, JOE!" Ben yelled, "wait for me. Are you going over to see the fun?"

"What fun?" Joe asked when Ben caught up with him. "I'm going to hear that fellow Paul preach."

"That's what I mean," Ben said. "They sure are exciting meetings. Did you hear about last night? Some of the fellows were going to run Paul out of town for saying that we Jews are sinners just like any dog of a Gentile."

"Phooey!" Joe exclaimed. "Why is that such a terrible thing to say? We *are* sinners, aren't we?"

"Well sure, stupid," Jim said uncertainly, "but we're God's special friends; we can sin if we want to and God doesn't care. Don't you remember what God promised Abraham? He told him He'd give Abraham the whole wide world."

"Stupid yourself," Joe said, "because that isn't all He said. He said He would bless those who obey Him. That means if we don't obey Him it's all off."

"Well, in that case we're all as good as lost," Ben said thoughtfully, "because all of us have sinned. I wonder if that's what Paul meant last night when he said that God will punish us Jews for our sins and that Jesus Christ came to save us and died for us? Come on, hurry up, I want to hear what he's got to say."

Would you like to read part of the sermon Paul might have been preaching that night? Listen carefully, because here it is.

2:1-16

[1] "Well!" you may be saying. "What terrible people those others are that you have been talking about." But wait a minute! Have you ever stopped to think that you are just as bad? When you say they are bad and should be punished, you are talking about yourself, for you are doing some of the very same things. [2] And God will surely punish anyone who does such things, even you. [3] Don't think that God will forever punish other people who do these things, and then let you get by; don't imagine that you will somehow escape God's terrible anger when you are doing them too.

[4] Does this make you smile? "God hasn't punished me yet," you say. Do you think this proves He won't? Can't you see that God is so kind that He is eagerly trying to help you? He has waited so long before punishing you because He is hoping that if you are given enough time, you will turn away from the bad things you are doing and come to Him. [5] But with your hard heart and your unwillingness to come to God, you are saving up terrible punishment for yourself; for there is going to come a day when God will be the Judge of all such people and [6] will pay them terrible wages for whatever evil they have done.

⁷ He will give eternal life to those who patiently do whatever God tells them to, so that they can have glory and honor, and live forever. ⁸ But He will terribly punish those who fight against God and won't obey Him, but obey Satan; God's anger will be poured out upon them. ⁹ There will be sorrow and torture for everyone who keeps on sinning, no matter whether he is a Jew or a Gentile (or whether he is a Protestant or a Roman Catholic or goes to any other church or to no church at all).* ¹⁰ And God will give glory and honor and peace to all alike who obey Him. ¹¹ For God treats everyone the same, no matter what their race or color.*

¹²ᵃ God will punish sin, no matter who does it. ¹⁴ Those who never had God's laws written out for them will perish anyway for disobeying them, because they know in their hearts what is right and wrong, and the laws are written inside them. ¹⁵ They know when they are sinning, and nobody needs to tell them. So God is going to punish them for their disobedience.

¹²ᵇ You Jews, to whom God gave the Ten Commandments, will perish because you don't do what they say to do. ¹³ After all, you aren't saved by *knowing* what you should do, but by *doing* it.

¹⁶ The day will surely come when God will have Jesus Christ judge the secret lives of everyone, for this is all part of God's great plan just as I have taught it to you.

SOME QUESTIONS TO ANSWER:

1. Why did the Jews become so angry with Paul and want to kill him?
2. Does God save people if they go to church and try to be good? What is God's plan for getting people into heaven even though they deserve hell?
3. If you are born in a Christian home and have a Christian father and mother, does that make you a Christian too? How does a person get saved who is born in a Protestant

*This is the current application and amplification of Paul's thought.

home? What about a Roman Catholic home? What about a Jewish home?

4. There is a "little voice" inside you to help you know what is right and wrong. What is the "little voice" called?

5. What happens to the "little voice" if you keep disobeying it?

A PRAYER

Our Father, thank You for Your patience with us, and thank You for Jesus, who died to take away my sins. Thank You for my conscience, that helps keep me from sinning. Please help me to listen to whatever You tell me and to quickly do all You say. In Jesus' name. Amen.

6

Your Rich Uncle Can't Help You

PAUL WOULD BE GLAD if he were alive today because of the way that some of his Jewish relatives are becoming interested in the Lord Jesus Christ. *The Sunday School Times* tells about Mr. George T. B. Davis, who for many years has been giving thousands of New Testaments to Jews in America and other parts of the world. Mr. Davis says, "In Miami Beach where there are thousands of Jewish people during the winter season, we gave three lectures and about nine hundred Jews attended the meetings; to our amazement and delight some five hundred of them—over half of those present—asked for copies of the New Testament. Reports from other countries we visited indicate that the interest of the Jews in the Word of God is becoming greater and greater."

But long ago when Paul offered the message of the New

Testament to the Jews, they wouldn't take it at all. They thought they were already saved because of being special friends of God and relatives of Moses and King David and Solomon. But in Paul's letter he reminds them that they too are lost and without God and need a Saviour. He is trying to wake them up. Listen as we read and see if you think he does a good job.

2:17-27

17 Listen to me, you who are Jews! You think you will be saved because you have learned the Ten Commandments. You brag that God loves you more than anyone else. 18 You know His laws and what He likes. You can tell anyone what is right to do and what is wrong. 19 You are sure you can show people how to get God to like them if they don't know how; you think you are a sort of light so people can follow you through the dark to God. 20 You think you are great teachers and that everyone else is stupid. You say you know how to teach even babies what is right and what God wants, because you know God's laws so well.

21 But what I say is that you are the ones who need a teacher to tell you what to do. You like to tell other people that they shouldn't steal, and then you steal things yourselves. 22 You say not to marry a person who is already married, and then do it yourselves. You say that other people must worship only God and then you worship money.

23 You brag about knowing what God wants you to do, and yet you don't do it, but dishonor God by breaking His laws. 24 Don't you realize that it is because of you and the way you act that other people hate God? They say, "Well, if that's the way God's people are, I certainly don't want to be one of them."*

25 It doesn't make a bit of difference about your being born as a Jew, one of God's chosen people, if you do not obey God. You're lucky to be a Jew and to know God's laws if you are going to obey them. But if you know them and don't obey them, you are no better off than the people who never heard

*Implied.

them in the first place. ²⁶ And remember this: a person who isn't a Jew but obeys God's laws, will be given all the rights a Jew has. ²⁷ In fact, he is much better than you Jews who know so much about God but haven't obeyed Him; so your sin is greater than theirs.

SOME QUESTIONS TO ANSWER:

1. Did the Jews there in Rome think they needed a Saviour? Why not?
2. If people *know* what God wants them to do, does that get them into heaven?
3. Did the Jews know God's laws? Did they obey them? Could they obey all of them? Then how could they get to heaven?
4. What will people think about God if we are His children and misbehave?

A PRAYER

Our Father, we pray today for Your people, the Jews. Thank You that many of them are beginning to understand about Jesus and want Him as their Saviour. Help the many others to understand also. And please help us as Your children to live good lives so that we can bring honor to You and so that we will not turn people away from loving You. In Jesus' name. Amen.

7

What's the Use of Living in a Christian Home?

JACK WASN'T A CHRISTIAN but he thought he was.

"Why don't you become a Christian?" someone asked him one day.

"Why, I am a Christian," Jack said in a hurt sort of voice.

"You are?" his friend asked, surprised. "When did you become one?"

"I was just born a Christian," Jack said, "because my mother and father are Christians."

"But that doesn't help *you* any," his friend said. "You've got to decide for yourself."

"Decide what?" Jack asked, feeling uneasy.

"Decide whether you want your sins to be put over onto Jesus, whether you want Him as your Saviour," the friend told him quietly.

And Jack's friend was right. You aren't saved by what your

parents believe. When *you* believe, *then* Jesus will wash away *your* sins.

But does that mean it isn't important to be born in a Christian home? Oh, no, it doesn't mean that at all, for children who aren't born in Christian homes usually never learn about Jesus and His love. How you should thank God every day for letting you be born in a Christian family instead of in some far-off land where the name of Jesus has never even been heard of.

Today in his letter, Paul is talking again to the Jews who think they are all right because of their families. Listen now to what Paul says to them.

2:28—3:8

28 You are not a real Jew just because your father and mother are, or because you have gone through a Jewish ceremony as a sign that you belong to God. 29 No, a real Jew is anyone who sets his heart to obey God and wants to do whatever God says. The way to God is not by going through a Jewish ceremony, but by a change inside us. Then we are God's chosen people, and God will praise us and save us, even though other people think we are fools.

1 "Then what's the use of being born a Jew?" you might ask. "The Bible is full of promises to us as His special people. Aren't we going to be saved in some special way?"

2 There are many advantages in being a Jew. One of the most important is that we Jews were given the words of God so that we could know His will. 3 And the advantage was still there even though some of the Jews didn't want to obey God. Was God telling a lie then, when He promised salvation to the Jews, and they turned it down? 4 Of course not! Though everyone else in the world is a liar, God is not. Remember what it says in the book of Psalms, that His words will always prove to be true if anyone challenges them.

5 "But," you might say, "our sins help God because people will notice how good God is when they see how bad we are.

So it isn't fair for Him to punish us for our sins, when our sins really help Him!" (I hope you clearly understand that I'm using other people's arguments here, not my own.)

⁶ God forbid that they should say such a terrible thing. If God acted that way, then what kind of a God would He be, and how could He ever condemn anyone? ⁷ For if it were true that my lies glorify God by showing everyone how honest He is, then God could never condemn me as a sinner; but He does. ⁸ If you follow out that idea, what you come to is that the worse we are, the better God likes it—and some people even say that I have taught them such things. Such people richly deserve the judgment that awaits them.

⁹ Well then, what is the conclusion of this whole matter? It is that God's people, the Jews, are no better than anyone else and don't have any special way of being saved. We are all sinners, and we all need the same Saviour.

SOME QUESTIONS TO ANSWER:

1. What does Paul mean by saying that a person isn't a real Jew just because his parents are Jewish?
2. What advantage is there about being born into a Christian home?
3. What was the advantage of being born into a Jewish home?
4. Why did some people say that it is a good thing to sin and that this brings glory to God? What was Paul's answer?

A PRAYER

Our heavenly Father, please help us to realize that we are not Christians because we have been born into Christian homes, but only if we let Jesus save us. Help us to remember that Your promises are for those who give themselves to Jesus. Thank You for all the good things You have done for us and that You are going to do. In Jesus' name. Amen.

8
God's Way of Salvation Made Plain

"HERE IS A NICKEL," said Jon thrusting out a grimy hand toward Mommie who was washing dishes. "And what's it for, son?" she asked knowing well enough the problem he faced.

"Well, well, it's for that candy bar Jane and I took last night when we were doing dishes. I'm paying for it," he added a bit defiantly.

"But, Jon, that's not the point. It isn't the cost of the candy bar that matters to Mommie and Daddy, it's that you took it without asking; and paying the nickel won't change the fact that you took it. That's what made us feel so bad.

"We've forgiven you, but not because of your paying for it. And you see, Jon, it was that sort of thing which sent the Lord to the cross for us. We couldn't pay for the wrong we've done, and so He paid.

"And another thing, Jon. He not only paid for the taking of the candy bar, but He died to cleanse us from the sin in our hearts that even made us think of doing such a thing. He forgives—and He cleanses our hearts.

"Daddy and Mommie can forgive you for taking the candy, but we can't do a thing about the sin in your heart. Have you asked the Lord to forgive you and to make your heart clean, Jon?"

His eyes filled; he nodded his head and turned to go up the back stairs. Mommie noted with thankfulness that the nickel was slipped into his pocket. "Lord, make it real to his heart that he can't pay for his own sin, and, oh, help him to see what it cost You to pay for it!"

—DORIS ALDRICH, *The Doorstep Evangel*

Today we are going to read some of the very most important words that have ever been written anywhere! For here in this part of his letter, Paul tells all his friends that they can never get to heaven by being good enough because they are *not* good enough. Instead, God has arranged a different road to heaven that really gets there. God's way to heaven is by going with Christ. He can get in and all His friends may come with Him. Are you one of His friends?

3:10-31

¹⁰ It is written in the Old Testament that no one is good enough to get to heaven by himself; no, no one anywhere in all the world. ¹¹ Not one has ever lived the way he should and always obeyed God. ¹² Everyone has been bad, and become worthless to God. Not one person anywhere has kept on doing what is right; no, not one. ¹³ They all say mean, dirty things.

They tell lies.

They enjoy saying things about other people to try to get them into trouble.

¹⁴ Their mouths are foul with cursing and bitterness.

¹⁵ They are quick to want to kill.

¹⁶⁻¹⁷ Wherever they go, they leave misery and wreckage behind them instead of peace.

¹⁸ And they don't care anything about God or what He thinks of them.

¹⁹ That is what God says to the Jews, and so they cannot claim that they are good, nor can anyone else. The whole world stands guilty before God.

²⁰ So you can see that no one anywhere will ever get to heaven by trying to be good enough. For when we know what God wants us to do, it only makes us realize how far short we come from doing it.

²¹ But now God has made a different way for us to get to heaven, and by this way we don't have to be good enough. It is the way the Bible tells about; and the old way that didn't work (of trying to be good enough) helps us see how much we need this new way. ²² This is the new way: God makes us good enough for heaven when we trust Jesus Christ to save us. Anyone, no matter who he is, can be saved this way.

²³ For all of us have sinned and come short of the glory of God. ²⁴ But now God gladly counts us as being good because of His kindness in forgiving our sins when Christ died for us. ²⁵ And now God is satisfied with us because of what Christ did to us who have faith in His blood.

The sins of God's friends in the Old Testament have been forgiven in this way, and are all gone because God was willing to wait for Christ to die for them. ²⁶ And God is able to forgive us today too; and so He is still a true Judge who does right even though he doesn't punish us for being bad if we have faith in Jesus.

²⁷ Can we brag then, that we have done so much good that God will let us into heaven? No, because we are saved by Jesus, not because we have been good enough. ²⁸ And so we see that a person gets to heaven by trusting Jesus, not by being good enough or doing good.

²⁹ And does God only save the Jews this way? No; all of us

get to heaven the same way. ³⁰ God is the same to all; all are saved the same way, by trusting Jesus.

³¹ And does this mean that we don't have to be good any more? Oh, no; this way God can make us *really* good.

SOME QUESTIONS TO ANSWER:

1. Has there ever been anyone besides Jesus who has never done anything wrong?
2. If a person has ever done one thing wrong, is he good enough to get to heaven? Have you ever done anything wrong? Are you good enough to go to heaven?
3. How did God arrange it so that you could get there?

A PRAYER

O God, how can we thank You enough for saving us when we were so bad? Help us to understand how much our Lord Jesus went through because of us. Help us to love Him very much because of all that He has done for us; and thank You again for making a way for us to escape from the wrath of God against our sins. In Jesus' name. Amen.

9

Saved
Some
Other
Way?

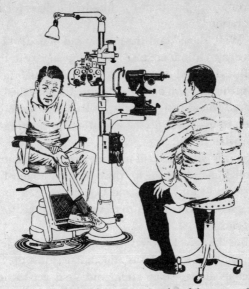

A MAN WAS HAVING A LOT OF TROUBLE with his eyes. His doctor examined him carefully and then shook his head. "My friend," he said, "you are in trouble. There is only one doctor anywhere near here who can help you. It is going to take a very difficult and expensive operation to make your eyes well." The doctor wrote down a name and address on a piece of paper and gave it to the man. "Here is the name of the doctor who can help you," he said. "I would advise you to go at once and take plenty of money with you, for it's going to cost you a lot."

The man had eighty dollars in the bank, so he got his money and went to see the other doctor. After examining his eyes very carefully, he said, "Yes, you need the operation, and in a hurry. And I am not sure you can pay what it will cost. I never accept less than five hundred dollars for this particular operation."

"Well, then," said the man in sad despair. "I guess I'll just have to go blind, because I have only eighty dollars."

But the good doctor said, "There is one other way to solve our trouble. You don't have enough to pay the bill, and I can't charge you as little as eighty dollars, but there is another way open to us—I will do the operation for nothing." And that is just what he did.

So it is with God and us. Not one of us has anywhere nearly enough money to pay for the operation on our hearts that will make us fit for heaven, and God cannot sell us the operation cheaply. So He gives it to us without charge, for Jesus died to pay our way.

But the Jews Paul was writing to didn't like Jesus and didn't think they needed Jesus and didn't think they needed help. "Let us alone," they said, "and we'll get to heaven by ourselves, just like Abraham did." They failed to realize that Abraham got there by the grace of God. So now in the part of the letter we will read today, Paul is talking about Abraham, for he was the first of all the Jews, and they all thought that whatever he did was the very best and that they should follow his example. Well, Paul asks, how did Abraham get to heaven? It wasn't because he was a Jew, for he hadn't been born a Jew or gone through the joining ceremony to become one. No, he was saved just like anyone else, by believing and trusting in God. He could never have paid his own way but he gladly accepted God's gift. Have you?

4:1-25

¹ How did father Abraham get to heaven? ² If it was be-

cause he obeyed all of God's laws, he would have something to boast about. But it wasn't that way at all. ³ What does the Bible say about him? It says that Abraham believed God's promises and God counted that faith to be as valuable as though he had never sinned. So you see, he was saved because He believed God's promises.

⁴ If we work hard for something, then when we finally get it, it isn't a gift, but it is something we have earned. ⁵ But that's not the way we get salvation. We do not get that by working for it, but by believing that Jesus died for our sins. God counts our faith instead of our sins. ⁶ King David was talking about this when he mentioned how happy a person is when God forgives him and makes everything all right, even though he doesn't deserve it.

King David said, ⁷ "Blessed, and to be envied, are those whose sins are forgiven, and all taken away. ⁸ Blessed is the man whose sins God doesn't count any more."

⁹ Now here is another important question. Does God only save the Jews who believe, or is it the same for you and me too? I ask this because the Bible says *Abraham* was saved by faith. Does it mean *only* Abraham and the Jews can be saved that way? ¹⁰ Well, *when* was Abraham saved? It was *before he became a Jew.* ¹¹ It wasn't until later on, *after* God had promised to bless him *because of his faith* that he went through the ceremonies that made him the first Jew. He went through the circumcision ceremony (and became a Jew) as a sign that God had already forgiven his sins. So now all the people who aren't Jews can see that the way for them to be saved is by believing, not by being circumcised and becoming Jews. God will gladly forgive their sins if they believe Him. ¹² And the Jews can see that they are not saved by a ceremony, but by believing, just as Abraham did.

¹³ So you see, God's promise to bless Abraham and the Jews wasn't because he knew God's laws and always did what he should, but because he trusted God to forgive him for the wrong things he had done. ¹⁴ And if you say that a person can only be saved by obeying the Ten Commandments, then you are saying that a person like Abraham (who did not even

know the Ten Commandments) was lost and that God's promises to him were no good.

¹⁵ If salvation depends on keeping all the laws, then we don't have a chance, and we will all be lost. But God did not give Abraham a lot of laws to keep in order to be saved, and so he was not lost when he didn't obey them.

¹⁶ God has said that He will save us if we trust Him, and not because we are good enough. That way we can be sure of our salvation, since God is giving it to us instead of our trying to earn it. This way, anyone can be saved, whether he is a Jew or anyone else, if he trusts in God as Abraham did, who is an example of people everywhere who have been saved by believing God.

SOME QUESTIONS TO ANSWER:

1. Did Abraham get to heaven because he was so good? How was he saved?
2. Did Abraham get to heaven because he was a Jew? Had he become a Jew yet?
3. Can you be saved by being good enough? Then how?

A PRAYER

Our Father, thank You for the Bible, and thank You that Paul wrote this letter that helps us understand how to be saved. We want to pray today for the Jews all over the world that they may be able to understand about these things too. Open their eyes and hearts that they might see and understand and be saved through Jesus Christ our Lord. Amen.

10

God Couldn't, But Did!

GOD WAS PLEASED when Abraham trusted him, and God was pleased when a Christian woman out in Africa asked Him for a strange gift.

You see, her baby was sick. The mother was a poor, ignorant woman who had become a Christian and knew that Jesus was her Friend.

It was several months after she asked Jesus to be her Saviour that her little child became sick. Everyone thought the baby was surely going to die. Ice was needed, but in all that hot country, there were no refrigerators and no ice anywhere.

"I am going to ask God to send ice," the mother said to one of the missionaries.

"Oh, no!" the missionary said sadly. "You can't expect Him to do that."

"Why not?" asked the simple-hearted believer. "He has all the power, and He loves me. You told me so. I shall ask Him, and I believe He will send it."

She did ask Him, and God answered. Soon there came a great thunderstorm with rain and hail pelting down. Joyfully thanking God, the happy mother ran out into the storm with a large bowl and scooped it full of icy hailstones.

God heard and answered her "impossible" prayer of faith.

Abraham was another one who always believed God, no matter how wonderfully impossible God's promises to him were. Today we will read about one of those strange promises. Do you think Abraham could believe it would actually happen? Let's read and find out.

4:17-25

[17] God promised to give Abraham many children and Abraham believed Him because he knew that God could even raise the dead and make things out of nothing.

[18] God said He would give Abraham a son who would have many children and become a great nation; and Abraham believed Him even though it just couldn't be!

[19] And because his faith was strong, he didn't worry about the fact that he was too old to be a father at the age of one hundred, and that Sarah, his wife, was too old to have a baby. [20] That didn't bother him; he went right ahead and believed God and gave glory to God even before it happened!

[21] He knew God would do whatever He promised, [22] and because of this, God forgave Abraham's sins. [23] Now this wonderful promise—that he would be saved through his faith—wasn't just for Abraham's benefit. [24] It helps us too, telling us that God will save us the same way, by our believing the promises of God who brought Jesus back to life again: [25] Yes, Jesus who died for our sins, and whom God brought back to life so that He could make us fit for heaven.

SOME QUESTIONS TO ANSWER:

1. How old was Abraham when God told him that he and Sarah would have a baby?
2. Why did he think Sarah would have a baby when he knew she was too old?
3. What did God think about Abraham's faith?
   What does He think about your faith?
4. A thought question: How can you learn to trust God more?

A PRAYER

Dear Lord Jesus, help us to trust You more and more. We know that You want to do great things for us, and that sometimes You can't because we don't ask You to or don't really think You will. But, Lord, we know You can. Help us to believe. Thank You for Abraham and the way he trusted You, and help us to trust You, too. In Jesus' name we ask this. Amen.

11
The
War
Is Over!

WHEN WE WANT TO FIND OUT how much gasoline there is in the car, we look at the gauge on the dashboard. And if we want to know whether a person is happy or angry or sad down inside, we look at his face and it usually tells us. I want to tell you about the face of Adoniram Judson, one of the first missionaries, who went to Burma to tell the people there about Jesus. But the people of Burma weren't interested in Jesus and treated Mr. Judson cruelly. For a while they put him in a terrible jail where they tortured him every night and left him in chains all day. When, at last, he came home to visit America after terrible years away, a small boy watched him coming off the ship and recognized him from a picture he had seen in the newspaper.

The boy ran up the street to where his pastor lived to tell

him about it and the pastor hurried back with him. Yes, the boy was right. It was Adoniram Judson. The minister was soon talking with the missionary and forgot all about the boy who had brought him the news, but the boy stood there silent and eager, unable to tear himself away from that wonderful face. Even after all Mr. Judson had been through, peace and love and joy were in his face and in his heart. He was trusting God more than ever before.

Many years afterwards, that boy, Henry Clay Trumbull, became a famous minister himself and editor of *The Sunday School Times* magazine. He wrote a book in which there was a chapter called "What a Boy Saw in the Face of Adoniram Judson."

What do people see in your face? Do they see the joy of the Lord, or is your face grim or sad or angry because you don't realize all the wonderful things God has done for you? Paul's letter today tells us about some of these great things. Let's read it now.

5:1-11

¹ So, since we have been made right in God's sight by faith in His promises, not by our trying real hard to be good, we can now have real peace with God because of what our Lord Jesus Christ has done for us.

² It was Jesus who made it possible for us to have this happiness of being God's children; and we know too how good He is going to be to us in the future; and we know about the glorious things He is preparing for us.

³ But it's not only the nice things He gives us that we can be happy about. We can be glad too when we run into problems and trials, because we know that these are really very good for us, and help us learn to be patient. ⁴ The troubles teach us to keep on trusting God until He gets us out of the trouble and shows us what to do. And when we see that He

always helps us if we wait, then we will trust Him even more the next time, and we will begin to have a steady hope and faith.

⁵ Then we will hold up our heads and know that all is well, no matter what other people think about us or do to us, for we will know that God loves us dearly and the Holy Spirit, whom God sent to help us, makes us feel this warm love everywhere in our hearts.

⁶ Oh, how wonderful God's love for us is!* Just to think that Christ died for us sinners when we couldn't help ourselves at all. ⁷ We wouldn't expect anyone to offer to die to rescue us even if we were good, though of course it is possible that someone might. ⁸ But God showed how much He loved us, when Christ died to rescue us while we were terribly bad.

⁹ And it is clear that God will never punish us now for our sins, because He has taken them away through Christ's blood and now declares us good. ¹⁰ And since God saved us when we were His enemies, by slaying His Son for us, it is surely easy for Him to keep us now, that His Son is alive again and we are His friends.

¹¹ What's more, now we can be full of joy instead of terrible fear when we think of God, because we are God's friends, and not His enemies—all because of what our Lord Jesus Christ has done for us.

SOME QUESTIONS TO ANSWER:

1. There is an old saying that big storms make strong trees because their roots go down deep to hold them up straight. Paul says that the problems we have are good for us. Can you explain why?
2. If you had to die for someone else, would you rather die for a good friend or for someone who is bad?
3. Did Christ die for you when you were bad, or after you had become His good friend?
4. Does your face show that God has rescued you from hell and given you a ticket to heaven? Discuss: Is it an insult

*Implied.

46

to God for a Christian to be sour and unhappy? How can Christians be happier?

PRAYER

Thank You, Lord Jesus, that we are Your children. Thank ou for loving us and taking care of us. May people see the joy f the Lord Jesus Christ in our faces and be attracted to Him ecause of our smiles. In Jesus' name. Amen.

12

Death
Had to
Die!

Mr. La Guardia, one of the famous mayors of New York City, used to be a judge at a police court. One day a trembling old man was brought before him, charged with stealing a loaf of bread. The old man said that he had to do it because his family was starving.

"Well, I have to punish you," said Mr. La Guardia. "The law makes no exception, and I can do nothing but sentence you to a fine of ten dollars."

Then he added, after reaching into his pocket, "And here's the ten dollars to pay for your fine."

"Furthermore," he said, as he threw another dollar into his hat, I'm going to fine everyone in this courtroom fifty cents for living in a town where a man has to steal bread in order to eat."

So he passed the hat around, and the man, with the light of heaven in his eyes, left the courtroom with $47.50.

Isn't this a very tiny picture of what Christ has done for us? Today Paul's letter tells about how our Lord paid the terrible death penalty for our sins, dying in our place; and then besides all that, He has given us eternal gifts. What a wonderful Saviour!

5:12-21

¹² When Adam disobeyed God, God said that he must die, and so it was that death came into the world by Adam. That day God changed Adam and all his children into people with dying bodies. That is the reason why you and I must die some day too, because we have all been infected with Adam's sin and our bodies were born damaged by his sin.

^{13-14a} We know it is because of Adam that we die, and not because of our own sins, because in the long years between Adam and Moses, God hadn't told the people what His law was, so He didn't kill them for disobeying. When they died, it wasn't for their own sins, and it wasn't because they had done the same things Adam did wrong, for their sins were different from his. No it was *not* because of the bad things *they* did that they died, but because they had been hurt by what Adam did.

^{14b-15a} Adam is like Christ in some ways. Each gave something to all the world. But, oh, what different things they gave!* ^{15b} Adam's sin gave all of us the gift of *death*, but God in great kindness gives everyone the gift of abounding *life*, because of what Jesus Christ did.

¹⁶ And here is another great difference between Adam and Christ: Adam's *one* sin brought death to many, while Christ freely takes away *many* sins and gives glorious life instead.

¹⁷ It is a strange and mysterious thing* the way the sin of this one man, Adam, caused death to come upon all of us. But what a far greater miracle it is* that all who will accept

*Implied.

49

God's gift of forgiveness for their sins will win out by getting life from this one Man, Jesus Christ.

¹⁸ Yes, Adam's *sin* brought punishment to all, but Christ's *goodness* is offered to all so that they can be forgiven. God's gift of goodness more than overcomes Adam's sin unto death.

¹⁹ Adam caused many to be hurt because he *disobeyed* God, and Christ caused many to be saved because He *obeyed*.

²⁰ Then, long after Adam, came the Ten Commandments which God gave to Moses so that all of us could see on how many points we fail and have sinned as a result of what Adam did to us. But as we see our sins more clearly, we can also see that there is enough of God's grace to forgive them all.

²¹ And so we see that sin brought death to be our king, but Jesus Christ our Lord won out and has made His kindness rule over us instead. He has made us right with God and has given us eternal life.

SOME QUESTIONS TO ANSWER:

1. Who were the first people ever to sin? What did God say would happen to Adam because of this?
2. How did Adam's sin affect his children?
3. Why do babies sometimes die even though they are not old enough to sin? Do they die for their own sins? Whose sin has caused them to have dying bodies?
4. What did Christ do about Adam's sin? Since the guilt of Adam's sin has been wiped away from everyone, including babies, and the babies are too young to sin, what happens to them when they die?

A PRAYER

O Lord God, how can we Thank You enough for all that You have done for us? Thank You so much for taking away our sins, and for giving us wonderful gifts. Help us now to live for You, and not for ourselves. Help us to tell others about the great things You want to do for them, and may they become Your children too. In Jesus' name. Amen.

13
Fatal Attraction

LAST CHRISTMAS I saw some children playing an interesting game with toy automobiles. The little toy men in the cars who were driving them were holding the steering wheels tightly trying to go straight ahead, but instead the cars were moving around all over, even backing up and sometimes bumping into each other. Can you guess why? Because the boys who were playing with them were holding magnets under the top of the table, right under the plastic cars, and there was a chunk of metal inside each car. So the cars on top of the table moved wherever the magnets moved under the table. That is the way the boys made the cars go wherever they wanted them to. The little drivers inside had to go where the magnet went, not where they wanted. The only way they could have helped themselves would have been to throw out the piece of metal in the car and then they would have been freed from the power of the magnet. Then they could go where they wanted to instead of where the magnet pulled them.

Do you see how this illustration applies to us Christians? Christ got rid of something in us that always went wherever Satan told it to go, so now we are free to follow Christ wherever He wants us to go. Now Christ can protect us from the pull of Satan's power. Now we can keep from sinning by letting Christ help us.

6:1-11

¹ Now don't get the wrong idea. Some people are actually saying that we ought to keep on sinning after we become Christians so that God will have an opportunity to be kind to us and forgive us, as He loves to do. ² Oh, what a terrible thought! How could we ever want to live in sin any longer now that we have become Christians, hating all that sort of thing? If you are really a Christian you are deadened against sin—you no longer want to keep on sinning. ³ Don't you know that when you took Christ as your Saviour, He fatally wounded the old desire to sin that you were born with? ⁴ Yes, your old wanting-to-do-bad-things was, so to speak, buried with Jesus. And when God gloriously brought Christ back to life, you were given in its place a wonderful new life inside you that makes you hate sin.

⁵ Yes, we are part of Christ,* and so when He died, our old sinful self lost control; and then when Christ came back to life, we were given a new life to take control inside us.

⁶ Our old evil desires were crucified with Christ; this part of us that loved sin was crushed when we accepted Christ,⁷ and now that this has happened, Satan can't make us serve him anymore. ⁸ This old life of sin has been wounded unto death by Christ, and Christ gave us His own life to be ours inside us. ⁹ And when Christ died and rose again to deliver us from Satan's power,* once was enough and sin was forever

*Implied.

52

subdued. It can never conquer us again. [10] He died only once for our sins, but now He lives forever with God.

[11]So that is why you can be free from your old desires; they have lost their grip and you are free in the Lord through what Christ has done.

SOME QUESTIONS TO ANSWER:

1. When we became Christians, what happened to Satan's terrible grip that he had on us? Who is it who keeps him away?
2. Discuss: the part of us Satan once controlled is sick and weak, but we can feed it and make it strong and ask it to rule over us again. How do we feed this old nature?
3. If we have let it grow strong again, is there anything we can do about it? See I John 1:9.

A PRAYER

Our heavenly Father, help us to understand the wonderful thing that You did when You died for us and killed the power of Satan over us. Thank You that we no longer have to obey him. Thank You that the part of us that he could always control is dead, and that instead You have given us a wonderful new life that wants to live for God. In Jesus' name. Amen.

14

Danger!
Keep Away!

An American soldier wanted to teach a Christian native out in the Solomon Islands how to gamble. "Me no got any hands," said the Christian boy in his broken English.

"What do you mean?" asked the puzzled white man. "You have two hands."

"No, me no got hands," the boy insisted. "You see two hands, but they no my hands—they belong Jesus."

This boy was following Paul's advice to be a slave to Jesus and not to Satan anymore. He was free from Satan and didn't plan to get caught in Satan's web again.

It's up to you! The jail door is open and you can go out if you want to. You were chained to Satan but God cut you loose and set you free, so now should you still listen to Satan? Of course not! Yet some people do! After Christ has saved them they still go back where Satan is and try to sin just a little bit and hope it won't hurt them; and Satan is right there waiting to snatch them back into his great power.

Christ has made you free. He will keep you free if you let Him.

6:12-23

¹² So do not let Satan be king of your life anymore. Do not obey him anymore, with all his wicked thoughts and suggestions.

¹³ We must not step back into the old life where Satan can use us for his sinful purposes, but we must give ourselves entirely to God, because now we are alive to all that is good; let every part of you do good things for Him. ¹⁴ Satan must not ever have you again. It used to be hopeless, trying to do what is right, because you weren't strong enough to fight Satan, but now you have all of God's kindness and grace to help you.

¹⁵ Do you see, then, why it is so wrong and foolish to ask whether it would be all right to sin, now that we are Christians? "We aren't saved by being good," such people say, "We are saved by the blood of Christ. We are not under law, but under grace." May God have mercy on their souls. ¹⁶ Don't they know that if they keep right on serving Satan, it is because they still belong to him? But if they want to obey God, it is because they are His children.

¹⁷ How I thank God that although you were slaves to Satan, you have heard the gospel and believed it, and now your hearts want to do God's will only. ¹⁸ God made you free from Satan's power, and you have become slaves to doing good. ¹⁹ I am talking this way, about being slaves, because it makes it easy to understand: just as you used to let yourself be a slave to all kinds of sin, so now let yourself be a slave to whatever is right and holy.

²⁰ Before you became a Christian, you didn't have to bother much about being good. ²¹ Well, what did you get out of it? Evidently not much. since you are even ashamed to think

about what you used to do. You know that instead of helping you, it ruined you. ²² But now you are free from the power of Satan and have become servants of God instead, and the benefits you get include holiness and everlasting life.

²³ For the wages of sin is death, but the gift of God is eternal life through Jesus Christ our Lord.

SOME QUESTIONS TO ANSWER:

1. What two kings can we choose from to be lord of our lives? Have you made your choice? (If not, Satan wins!)
2. How do you yield to mother or father when they want you to do something but you want to do something else?
3. How do you yield to Christ?
4. Do you ever thank God for delivering you from Satan's terrible power? Perhaps that is something you will want to do in a prayer right now.

A PRAYER

Father in heaven, thank You for beating Satan off and letting us be free. Help me to serve only You forever. Help me not to let Satan come near, but to live safe in You. In Jesus' name. Amen.

15

Help That Didn't Help

A MAN PUT A BIG CHUNK OF MEAT into a pot and boiled it until it was soft enough to fall apart. Then he put two big forks into the meat, one on each side, to lift it out. But the meat was so soft that the forks tore right through it and the meat fell back into the pot. Then the man took a pancake turner and put it underneath the meat and that way he lifted it up and got it out.

God gave us His laws to obey and we can think of them as being like the forks and we are like the soft meat. God wanted to lift us up to heaven but we are soft with sin and so the laws God sent to help us weren't able to lift us up at all. Then God sent Jesus down to put His strong hands under us, and He lifts us up to glory. God's laws are good, but they cannot save us because we are too weak to keep them. Only Christ can lift us.

¹ Don't you understand yet, dear Jewish brothers in Christ, that you no longer need to fear the punishment in store for those who disobey the Ten Commandments?

Why?

Because you are dead! And a dead person isn't held responsible any more for obeying the laws. The law no longer has power or control over him.

² Let me illustrate this by an example of a woman who is married. She must obey her husband as long as he is alive. But if he dies, she doesn't need to anymore, because she is not married to him any longer. ³ Then she can even marry someone else if she wants to. That would be wrong when he was still alive, but it's perfectly all right after he is dead, for she is no longer married to him then.

⁴ And so, my brothers, you can see that the Ten Commandments used to be, so to speak, your "husband," or master, and you were therefore responsible to it. But when you accepted Christ as your Saviour, you died with Him on the cross, and, since you were dead, you were no longer married to the law, and it has no more power over you. Then you came back to life again when Christ did, and you are a new person; so now you are free to be married to someone else, to Christ, so to speak, and be fruitful in every good thing. . . .

⁶ Now we no longer need to try in vain to keep the law in order to be saved, because we are "dead" so far as the law is concerned; and now we can really serve God, not in the old way of a mechanical set of rules, but in the new way, with all of our hearts and minds.

⁷ Are God's laws then wrong and sinful, which He gave to the Jews in the Old Testament? Oh, of course not! No, the law is not sinful but it was the law that showed me my sin. I would not have known about the sin in my heart of wanting to steal unless the law had said, "You must not covet." ⁸ But Satan used the law against stealing to whisper that it was wrong and to make me want to do it all the more.

For if there were no laws, then we would not be so anxious to do what the law says is wrong. ⁹ That is why I felt fine until I heard what the law said. But when I heard all it said I must do to be saved, then I realized how hopeless it all was because I just couldn't do it. [10] So as far as I was concerned, the good law which was supposed to show me the way to heaven showed me instead that I couldn't get there that way at all, but that I was headed for hell. [11] Sin fooled me by taking the good Ten Commandments and using them to make me guilty of death.

[12] So you see that the law itself is wholly right and good.

[13] But didn't the law cause my doom? How then can it be good? No, it was sin, devilish stuff that it is, that used what was good to cause your death. Thus you can see how cunning and deadly and damnable a thing sin is.

[14] The law is good. The trouble is not there, but with me because I am too sinful to obey it.

SOME QUESTIONS TO ANSWER:

1. Is the law a bad thing or good?
2. Why can't we get to heaven by always obeying all the Ten Commandments?

A PRAYER

Dear Lord Jesus, thank You for making us free from Satan's power. Thank You for making us want to do what is good. Thank You most of all that we don't have to work our way to heaven, because we know we could never get there that way. Thank You for loving us so much that You died for us and took away our sins so that we can live with You forever. In Jesus' name we pray. Amen.

16
Who
Is
the Boss?

A BOY HAD THE RIGHT ANSWER whenever Satan came around to ask him to do something bad. "I don't talk to Satan about it," the boy said, "that way Satan can't get near me. Whenever he comes and knocks on the door to try to talk to me, I ask Jesus to answer the door and He does, and when Satan sees Jesus standing there he runs away real fast."

Three people live inside of you. One is you and one is God and one is sin. God wants you to do right, you want to do right, and sin wants you to do wrong. But Satan is stronger than you are. He can make you do wrong and you can't stop him by yourself. You are far too weak, but Christ is far stronger than Satan and sin and He is just waiting for you to ask Him to help you.

¹⁵ I can't figure out what's the matter with me. I want to do what is right, but I can't. I go right ahead and do things that are wrong, even though I hate myself for it.

¹⁶ I know perfectly well that I am doing wrong and that the laws I am breaking are good ones. ¹⁷ But I can't help myself. I'm not the one who is doing it. Sin inside me is stronger than I am, and it makes me do these things. ¹⁸ For I know that I am rotten through and through. No matter which way I turn, I can't seem to find how to do right, as I really want to.

¹⁹ Yes, when I want to be good I can't, and when I try not to be bad I am anyway. ²⁰ Now if I am doing what I don't want to, it's plain that the trouble is that sin still has me in its evil grasp, ²¹ so that I can't get away, and it says "no" when I want to do what is right.

²² Yes, I know what is right, and I want to do it. ²³ But there is something else deep inside me that is at war with my mind and wins the fight and makes me a slave to sin and death. In my mind I want to be God's willing servant, but instead I find myself tied fast to sin.

²⁴ Oh, what a terrible thing this is! Who will free me from this slavery to sin and death that is everywhere within me? ²⁵ Thank God! Jesus Christ our Lord will save me. He will set me free.

So you see how it is; the new life within me wants to serve God; but the old wounded, sinful nature, that is still present inside, loves Satan. But Christ will always help me when I trust Him to.

SOME QUESTIONS TO ANSWER:

1. Did Paul know what was right and wrong? Did he do what he should?
2. Who helped him?
3. What did the boy in the story do when Satan knocked?
4. When you feel the urge to do something wrong, what are some of the ways of getting away from Satan?

A PRAYER

O Lord Jesus, thank You for delivering us from the power of Satan and for helping us to be kind and good. Help us to always live for You and never to let Satan have his way with us again. In Jesus' name. Amen.

17

Whom Will You Vote For?

"Mother," said Mr. Bell, "today is Election Day. Let's be sure to remember to go down and vote."

Later that morning Mr. and Mrs. Bell went over to the place where the voting was going on. They were each given a paper to mark telling which man they wanted for President of the United States. And that night they sat up late watching TV to see who had won the election.

Do you know that there is an election every Christian must vote in, and he is the only person voting? So whomever he votes for wins. I am talking about electing the captain of our hearts. Who will it be, Satan or Christ?

Paul explains in his letter today what will happen if you vote for Satan and what will happen if you vote for Christ:

¹ There is no punishment awaiting those who belong to the Lord Jesus. ² For the life-giving power of the Holy Spirit—and this power is mine through Christ Jesus—has freed them from the grasp of sin and death. ³ It wasn't by trying to obey the Ten Commandments that I was lifted out of sin's grasp, because I couldn't and didn't keep them. Then God did something else that saved me. He sent His own Son, in a human body that could sin* just like mine, and destroyed sin's control over me by giving Himself as a sacrifice for my sins.

⁴ And now I can obey the law if I follow after the Holy Spirit and no longer seek to obey Satan. ⁵ Those who let themselves keep on following their old sinful desires find themselves breaking all the laws of God; those who follow after the Holy Spirit find themselves doing those things which are right. ⁶ Following after the Holy Spirit leads to life and peace, but following after sin and its ways lead to death, ⁷ because the old sinful mind inside us is against God. It never did obey God's laws, and it never will.

⁸ Therefore those who are still under the control of their old sinful self can never please God. ⁹ But you are not like that. You are ruled by the Holy Spirit, if you are a Christian, and the Spirit of God is inside you. (Remember that if anyone doesn't have the Holy Spirit, he is not a Christian at all.)

¹⁰ And even though Christ is in you, your body will still die because of sin; and your spirit will go to heaven because Christ has made it good.

¹¹ And the Holy Spirit, who raised up Jesus from the dead, lives in you and will make your dead body alive again too, after you die, if you are really a Christian and have the Holy Spirit living inside you.

¹² So your job is certainly not to be kind to your old sinful nature by doing what it begs you to. ¹³ For if you keep on following it, you are lost; but if through the power of the Holy Spirit, you crush out the bad things that Satan wants you to do, you will live.

*but never did, even once.

SOME QUESTIONS TO ANSWER:

1. What happens if we vote for Satan?
2. What happens when we vote for Christ?
3. How does the Holy Spirit help Christians overcome evil?

A PRAYER

Lord Jesus, we do love You and want You to rule over us and be our King. But we need Your help to keep us from temptation and from straying away from You and listening to our great enemy, Satan, who hates us. Lord, it is strange that we should want to follow him when we have You. We are weak and full of sin. Help us, we ask in Your mighty name. Amen.

18

Some Gifts God Has for You

A KING'S SON CAME RIDING down the street on a beautiful gray horse his father had given to him as a birthday present. Suddenly the horse became frightened and started running and plunging. A little boy stood in the way, too scared to move. The king's son leaped off the rearing horse and knocked the little boy out of the way, but the horse's hoofs came down on the little prince instead and he lay there dead.

I suppose you might think that the king was very angry with the boy who caused the death of his son, but instead he sorrowfully sent for the boy and adopted him into his own family to be the brother of the boy who was dead. And then, although the boy had been poor, he owned everything that belonged to the king's son.

Can you see why you are like the poor boy who became the

king's son? You were poor but God's Son died to save you, and now God has asked you to share in all of His Son's great wealth. Listen now as Paul tells us more about it.

8:14-27

[14] Just think! We are God's children if we have His Holy Spirit within us, telling us what to do. [15] Now we obey God, not because we are slaves who fear what He might do to us if we don't, but because we are His very own children and want to do whatever our dear Father tells us to.

[16] And His Holy Spirit speaks to us deep in our hearts and tells us that we are the children of God.

[17] And since we are His children, then we will share His treasures, and all that God has given to His Son, Jesus, is ours. Sometimes He lets us share in the sufferings of Jesus too, and have troubles and sorrows. But as a result, we will also share in His glory. [18] And the sufferings will be small compared to the wonderful things He is saving up to give us.

[19] For all creation is waiting patiently and hopefully for that day to come when God will glorify His children. [20] For on that day thorns and thistles and sin and death,* which overcame the world against its will at God's command, will all go away, [21] and all the world around us will share in the glorious freedom from the results of sin that the children of God are going to get.

[22] For we know that even the things God makes, like animals and plants, get sick and die. [23] And even we Christians, who have the witness of the Holy Spirit in us, still have plenty of troubles and are anxiously waiting for that coming day when God will give to us, His children, the new bodies He has promised us that will not be sick and that will never die.

[24] Having to wait for these wonderful things is good for us, better than if we had them now, for we are saved by trusting God, and having to wait for things helps us to trust Him more. If we already had them, then we wouldn't need to trust God to give them to us. [25] But if we have to keep trusting

*These specifics drawn from context and allusion.

Him for something that hasn't happened yet, it teaches us to wait patiently and confidently.

²⁶ And God has given us His Holy Spirit to help us with our problems while we are waiting. We don't even know what we should pray for, but the Holy Spirit prays for us with such feelings that they cannot be expressed in words. ²⁷ And the Father, who knows all hearts, knows, of course, what it is the Spirit is saying as He pleads for us for things that are God's will.

SOME QUESTIONS TO ANSWER:

1. What are some of the gifts God gives His children?
2. Do we get all His gifts now down here?
3. Does God keep away all troubles, sorrows, and problems from His children? Why?
4. Who does God send to help us when we have problems?

A PRAYER

O Father, thank You that we can call You Father, and that You love us so very much. Thank You for Jesus, who is our Brother, and who takes care of us and helps us. Please help us to love You as we want to, and to do whatever You tell us to, because You have done so much for us. In Jesus' name. Amen.

19
The Mighty Love of God for You

THERE WAS A GIRL who had two brothers. Someone asked her whether her mother loved her best or loved her brothers best. The girl very promptly replied, "She loves Jimmy best because he is the oldest, and she loves Johnny best because he is the youngest, and she loves me best because I am the only girl."

The girl was right. Her mother loved each one best of all.

And do you know that God loves *you* best? I hope you will remember this all your life. That is what Paul tells us about today as we read from his letter. Nothing that ever happens to His children can ever get them away from Him.

8:28-39

²⁸ We know that whatever happens to us is all right if we love God, and have accepted God's plan for our lives.

[29] For God decided long ago that when we would ask Him to save us, He would make us become like Jesus His Son; and so now God has us as His children right along with His first Son, Jesus. [30] And what's more, having decided this, He called to us to come to Him, and when we came, He declared us "not guilty" and filled us with Christ's goodness.

[31] What can we ever say to such wonderful things as these? If God is for us, who can be against us? [32] He did not even spare His own Son for us, but gave Him up for us all. Then won't He also surely give us freely everything else we need?

[33] Who dares to accuse us? Will God? No, He is the one who says we are all right. [34] Who can condemn us? Only Christ could—but He never will, because He is the one who died for us and came back to life again and is sitting there beside God in heaven, praying for us.

[35] What can separate us from the love of Christ? When we get hurt, is it because He doesn't love us anymore? Or when we are hungry, or don't have enough clothes, or are in danger, or even get killed? [36] No; these things may happen to us, because it says in the Bible that some of God's people will have a lot of trouble and face death. [37] But we are by far the conquerors of all these things because Jesus loves us still and helps us so much.

[38] I am sure that nothing can ever cut off His love from us. Death can't, and life can't. The angels certainly won't, and all the devils, and even Satan himself can't keep God's love away, nor things that have happened to us today or that are going to happen to us tomorrow, no matter where we are— [39] high above the sky, or in the deepest ocean—nothing will ever be able to separate us from the love of God which is in Christ Jesus, our Lord.

SOME QUESTIONS TO ANSWER:

1. What does Paul mean when he says that if God is for us no one can be against us?
2. If God lets us have a lot of troubles, does this mean that He doesn't love us anymore? Why would He let us have troubles if He loves us?

70

3. If we are following God's plan, can anything happen to us that He doesn't want to happen to us?

A PRAYER

Father in heaven, thank You for loving us all day long and all last night and that You are going to love us on and on for the rest of our lives. Thank You that You are not a god who is always trying to hurt us, but that You are always loving us and giving us good things. In Jesus' name. Amen.

20

Paul
Cries
for
His People

"WHY IS UNCLE JACK CRYING?" little Billy wanted to know.

"Because his cousin Barbara was hurt so badly in an accident," his mother told him.

Yes, sometimes even grown-up people cry. And Paul seems ready to cry as he writes this part of the letter. Why? Because his own friends and relatives, the Jews, won't come to Jesus. Paul knows that Jesus wants to save them but they won't come. So we can understand why Paul was so full of sorrow. We too should have sad hearts when we think of some of our friends who need Jesus so much and won't listen to Him.

9:1-15

¹⁻³ Oh, Israel, my people! Oh, my Jewish brothers! How I long for you to come to Christ, as I have. My heart is heavy within me. Sorrow has hold of me day and night because of

you. Christ knows, and the Holy Spirit knows, that I am not pretending when I say that I would be willing to be forever damned if that would save you.

⁴ God has given you so much, but still you will not listen to Him.* He asked you to be His special, chosen people and led you along with a bright cloud of glory and told you how very much He wanted to bless you. He gave you the Ten Commandments so that you would know what He wanted you to do. He let you work for Him in the temple. He gave you great promises if you would only listen and obey. ⁵ Great men of God were your fathers, and Christ Himself was One of you, a Jew, who now rules over all things and He is God, and blessed forever.

⁶ Were God's promises to you Jews no good then, since you are not being saved? No, not that. God didn't promise automatically to bless every Jew. ⁷ God gave these special promises to Abraham's son Isaac, but not to his other boys.

⁸ So you see that these wonderful promises to the Jews are not to all Jews, just because they happen to be born into Jewish families, but only to those Jews who trust God and believe His promises to them.

⁹⁻¹³ This is what God said to Abraham: "The son born to you next year is the one I have promised to bless." Later on, when this son Isaac grew up and married Rebekah,* God spoke again. He said, "I am going to give twin* boys to Isaac and Rebekah, and the one born first, named Esau, is going to grow up to be a servant to the other one, whose name will be Jacob. Yes, I will give my special blessing to Jacob, but not to Esau." This was not because one was good and the other bad, for, as I have said, the twins weren't even born yet when God said this. It was just that He wanted it that way.

¹⁴ Was God being unfair? Of course not. ¹⁵ God told Moses once, "If I want to be kind to someone, I will. And I will take pity on anyone I want to."

¹⁶ And so God's blessings are not given just because someone might like to have them, or tries to earn them. They are given to whomever He wants to have them.

*Implied.

73

1. Why was Paul so sad?
2. Did God promise to bless all of Abraham's children?
3. Will God save anyone who asks Him?

A PRAYER

O God, our heavenly Father, You are very great, and we are very poor and small. You have not looked down to see whether we deserve to be saved, but You have freely offered Your love to any of us who want to be saved. Thank You so much for all You have done for us, and help us to tell others the good news. In Jesus' name we ask these things. Amen.

21

Is It Fair?

ONE DAY A GREAT BARN caught on fire during a lightning storm. There were a hundred horses inside, but the men who took care of them quickly untied them and led them out into the barnyard where they could run away into the fields.

But as sometimes happens to horses when they get frightened, many of them dashed back into the barn when they smelled the fire, instead of running away from it.

The men took ropes and tried to lasso the horses as they were rushing back, and in that way were able to stop some of them and lead them out to safety. But many of the horses went back in and died in the terrible flames.

This true story may help illustrate part of what Paul is saying in his letter today: all have sinned and deserve eternal punishment. But God has chosen some of us to be kind to,

75

and captures us and pulls us back to be His children forever. He has not promised to save everyone, but He is always glad to receive anyone who wants to come to Him. He has never sent anyone away.

9:16-33

[16] God's blessings are not given just because someone might like to have them, or tries to earn them. They are given to whomever He wants to have them.

[17] An example of this was when God was talking to Pharaoh, the king of Egypt. God told him He had let him be the king just so He could make a terrible example of him for everyone to see what happens to people who don't obey God, and so everyone would know how great God is.

[18] So you see, God is kind to some people, just because He likes to be, and He hardens others so that they won't listen.

[19] Well, then, why does God blame them for doing wrong? Aren't they being the way God made them to be? [20] No, don't say that. You have no right to ask that question. Who are you to criticize God? Should the thing that is made say to the One who made it, "Why have you made me like this?" [21] When a man makes a jar out of clay, doesn't he have a right to use the same lump of clay to make one jar that is beautiful and will be used to hold flowers, and the other to throw garbage into?

[22] And so God has a perfect right to take people He has made and destroy them, after enduring them long and patiently, and in that way show His power and anger against their sins. [23-24] And He has a right to take other people such as ourselves, whether we are Jewish or Gentile Christians, and to be kind to us so that everyone can see how great His mercy and glory are, because that is why He made us.

[25] Remember what it says in the book of Hosea? "I will get me some other children from another family and love them even though they weren't part of my Jewish family." [26] And though God, in olden days, said the Gentiles were not His people, yet now He lets them become sons of the living God.

[27] Isaiah the prophet also said that only a few of the mil-

lions of Jews will be saved. [28] God will not keep waiting forever for them to come. He will soon punish them just as He promised. [29] Isaiah says in another place too that except for God's mercy, all the Jews would be destroyed—every single one of them—just as everyone was killed when God punished the cities of Sodom and Gomorrah.

[30] Well, then, what shall we say about these things? Just this, that God has made a way for the Gentiles also to be saved. [31] And the Jews, who tried so hard to be saved by keeping God's laws, were not saved. [32] Why not? It is because they didn't realize that they could only be saved by faith. When they tried to be saved by being good, they found it just couldn't be done.

They stumbled over a Rock in the road (and that Rock was Christ who had been sent to lift them up*). [33] The Old Testament tells about this when God said, "I am going to put a Rock in the path of the Jews and many will stumble over it. But all who use this Rock (that is, all who trust Jesus to save them) will surely be saved."

SOME QUESTIONS TO ANSWER:

1. What did Paul say to the people who wondered whether it was fair for God to save some people and not others?

2. Do you want Christ to be your Saviour? How can you come to Him?

A PRAYER

O God, we cannot understand why we have been chosen to receive such great things from You, but we do thank You very much. Help us to be truly thankful all the rest of our lives. And thank You that we are free to share this good news with others and that we have the privilege of inviting anyone we want to, to become Your children; for You have told us that we may pass on Your invitation to our friends so that they can come to You too. Help us to do this. In Jesus' name we ask it. Amen.

*Implied.

22

How to Be Saved

A MINISTER WAS INVITED to a party at the home of a very wealthy young man. Afterward the minister talked to him about God. "I'd like to be a Christian," the young man said, "if I only knew how."

"Well," said the minister, "suppose that the Lord Jesus stood there on the other side of the room and said, 'Come to Me. If you believe Me when I tell you that I died for you and want to save you, then you may come and follow Me.' "

"Then," said the young man, "I would go to Him and fall down before Him and ask Him to save me."

"But what if your friends were here in the room and they laughed at you?"

"I wouldn't care. I would go to the Lord Jesus."

"Well," said the minister, "the Lord Jesus is really in this room right now although you cannot see Him and He is stretching out His hands to you and saying, 'Come.' You should believe what He says in His letter, the Bible, just as though you heard the words from His own lips."

And the young man did come.

Have you come to Jesus? Have you brought others with you?

10:1-11

[1] Oh, my brother Jews, how I long for you; and how much I pray for you that you will be saved.

[2] Some of you are trying so hard to be saved, but you don't know the right way. [3] For you don't understand that Christ has died for you; you won't come to Him to save you. Instead you are trying to make yourselves good enough to be saved, by keeping the Ten Commandments. But that is not God's way of salvation. [4] You don't understand that the goodness Christ gives us is all that keeping the Ten Commandments ever hoped to finally get for us who trust Him.

[5] Moses said about being good, that if a person could be so good as to never once sin in all his life, he would be saved. [6-7] But when we are saved by faith, instead of by trying to be good enough, we can be saved right now, just by trusting Him and believing all that He has done for us.

We don't need to beg Christ to come down to us from heaven to save us, for He has already been here, nor beg God to make Him alive again, because God has already done that. [8] For salvation that comes from trusting Christ—which is what we preach—is within easy reach of each of us, in fact it is as near as our own hearts and mouths.

[9] For if we tell others that Jesus Christ is Lord, and if we believe in our hearts that God has raised Him from the dead, we will be saved. [10] For it is believing deep down inside that makes a man right with God; and then we must tell others that we have asked Jesus to save us.

SOME QUESTIONS TO ANSWER:

1. If a person wants to get to heaven by being good, and disobeys one of God's laws, is he good enough?
2. How good must one be to get to heaven?
3. Where can we find Christ to ask Him to save us?
4. How long must we beg Christ to save us before He will have pity on us?
5. What are some ways of telling others about Jesus?

A PRAYER

Our Father in heaven, help us to confess to others that we are Yours. We are so sinful still, and get embarrassed when we talk to others about You. Please help us not to be, but to feel at ease as we talk to them. And help us to live the kind of good lives that others will respect as we tell them about our Saviour. In Jesus' name we ask this. Amen.

23
Will You Be a Missionary?

An aged woman in India asked a missionary how long ago Jesus died for sinful people. "Look at me," she said, "I am old. I have prayed, given much money, gone to the idol temples and have become skin and bones by fasting so much. Where have you been all this time?"

An old Eskimo said to a missionary, "There have been many moons in this land. Did you know this good news then? Since you were a boy? And your father knew it too? Then why did you not come sooner?"

In Peru, a native asked, "How is it that all my life I have never before heard that Jesus spoke those precious words?"

A Bible seller in Casablanca was asked, "Why have you not run everywhere with this Book? Why do so many of my people not know the Jesus it tells about? Why have you kept it to yourselves?"

A missionary in Morocco was telling a woman the story of the love of Jesus, and when she had finished, the woman said, "It is a wonderful story. Do the women in your country believe it?"

"Yes," said the missionary, "of course."

After a moment's thought the woman said, "I don't think they do or they would not have been so long in coming to tell us."

Many are waiting for you to tell them of God's love and they will gladly come to Jesus when you do. It may cost you your life, but it will be well worth it. God says so. Listen as we read.

10:11-21

11 The Bible tells us that God will take care of everyone who believes on Jesus, 12 and that there is no difference between the Jew and the Gentile; the same Lord gladly gives His riches to all those who ask Him to save them. 13 Everyone, no matter who he is, who asks Jesus to save him will be saved.

14 But people can't ask Jesus to save them unless they believe in Him, and they can't believe in Him if they have never heard about Him. And how can they hear about Him unless you and I go and tell them?

15 And how will we go and tell them unless someone sends us? The Bible says, "How beautiful are those people who go and tell others about Christ and bring them glad news of the good things God has for them."

16 But how sad it is that everyone who hears the gospel won't believe in Jesus and obey Him. Isaiah the prophet said, "Lord, no one will believe me when I tell them."

17 How can we get people to believe it? It is when they hear

the Word of God. [18] But what about the Jews? Have they heard God's Word? Yes, for it has gone wherever they are. [19] And did the Jews know that God would give His salvation to others if they refused to take it? Yes, even 'way back at the time of Moses, God said that He was going to try to make the Jews angry and wake them up to what they were missing by giving the salvation they didn't want to other people. [20] And later on, Isaiah said boldly that God would be found by people who weren't even looking for Him, and they would be saved.

[21] In the meantime, He keeps reaching out His hands to the Jews to help them, but they keep refusing to come to Him.

SOME QUESTIONS TO ANSWER:

1. How can people call on the name of the Lord and be saved if we don't tell them about Him?
2. Which is more important, to make a lot of money, or to tell people about Jesus?
3. How does a person become a foreign missionary?
4. A hundred years from now, after you have died and gone to heaven, you will look back on your years in this life and wish that you had done only what God wanted you to do. Now you have a chance to do God's will, since your life is before you. Discuss how you can know what God wants you to be and do.
5. Will you give your life to God right now, or some other time today? If you haven't already done it, that will be one of the greatest decisions of your whole life.

A PRAYER

O God, who has taken away my sins and given me eternal life, I pray for Your help in giving my life back to You now. Use it as You will. Please send me, if You want to, to the far places of the earth to tell the people there about You. Help me to know that my life belongs to You and not to myself, and help me to joyously give it back for You to use in any way that You want to. In Jesus' name. Amen.

24

God's Invitation to the Jews

RIDING ALONG TOGETHER IN A BUS, a Christian in Jerusalem gave a New Testament to a Jewish preacher named Rabbi Slowstowski.

That evening the rabbi went up to his room in a hotel and began to read. He believed in God but not in the Lord Jesus. So before he started reading he prayed and asked God to help him to know the truth.

He kept on reading until three o'clock in the morning and then knelt down to pray. He cried out to God asking Him to show him what was right. Was the New Testament he was reading true after all? Was this strange story of Jesus really so? Was Jesus really God's Son?

Finally, for the first time in his life, he began to pray in the name of Jesus. He said afterwards that following this prayer there came into his heart such peace and joy as he had never known before. "Now I knew beyond any shadow of doubt that the Lord Jesus was the Messiah of the Jews and the Saviour of the world we had been looking for so long, and I accepted Him as my own personal Saviour. After this I went to bed, but I couldn't sleep. I was too full of joy and peace, and then I heard a real voice saying to me, 'Do not escape from Me anymore. I will use you to glorify My name and to be My witness.'

"Immediately I answered, 'Lord, here I am.' And from that time my life has not belonged to myself, but to Jesus. At first I wouldn't tell anyone, but soon I openly confessed Christ as my Saviour. Of course many friends turned against me, but this didn't bother me anymore, for I had the living Christ."

No, God has not turned away from all the Jews. Each day some of them are getting saved. That is the lesson Paul leaves with us today.

11:1-15

¹ Since the Jews have refused God's gift,* does this mean that God has become angry with them and thrown them all away? Oh, no, not at all! Remember that I myself am a Jew, a relative of Abraham's, and a member of Benjamin's family; ²⁻³ so you see, God has not thrown us all away. Do you remember what the Bible says about this? Elijah the prophet was telling God one day how the Jews had killed all the other prophets and torn up the places where people prayed and Elijah said that he was the only one left and that everyone was trying to kill him too.

⁴ And do you remember what God answered him?

God said, "No, you are not the only one left. I have seven thousand others besides you who still love Me and have not bowed to idols."

*Implied.

⁵ That is just the way it is now. Not all the Jews have turned away from God. There are a few who are being saved by taking God's wonderful free gift of salvation.

⁶ But of course they will only be saved by grace, not by trying to be good. God's salvation is a free gift, and can't be gotten by working to pay for it, or else it wouldn't be a gift anymore. You can't have it both ways. If you are trying to be saved by your hard work, then you can't have salvation free, for it isn't free if you have to buy it.

⁷ And so this is the way it is: most of the Jews have not found the Saviour they are looking for. A few have, the ones God has chosen, but the eyes of others have been blinded. ⁸ That is what the Old Testament is talking about where it says that God has made people to be asleep, shutting their eyes and ears for now so that they do not see or understand what we are talking about when we tell them about Christ.

⁹ And King David spoke of this same thing when he said that even the good food and other blessings of the Jews have trapped them into thinking everything is all right. ¹⁰ But their eyes are darkened so that they do not see that they are always walking with a heavy load.

¹¹ Did God do this for the purpose of bringing disaster to the Jews? Oh, no! His purpose was to get His salvation over to the Gentiles, and then the Jews would be jealous and begin to want God's salvation.

¹² Since the whole world became rich by getting God's offer of salvation after the Jews turned it down, think what even greater blessing the rest of the world will share in, later on, when the Jews also come to Christ.

¹³ As you know, God has made me a special messenger to the Gentiles. I tell the Jews about this whenever I can, ¹⁴ so that if possible, I can make them jealous; then some of them will get saved too. ¹⁵ And how wonderful it is when they become Christians! When God turned away from them, it meant that He turned to the rest of the world to offer His salvation; so now it is even more wonderful when some of the Jews are saved. It is like dead people coming back to life.

1. Has God given up all the Jews, so that none of them can be saved?
2. Can you think of two Jews who became Christians, whom we have just been reading about?

A PRAYER

O Lord, what shall we say to all these things, for You have given us all the blessings You were keeping for Your people, the Jews. Thank You that You are still waiting for them to come back to You, and we pray that soon they will understand about Jesus and take Him as their Saviour. Help us to remember to pray for them and to help them in every way we can. In Jesus' name we ask these things. Amen.

25

The Tree and the Branches

The Sunday School Times magazine told an interesting story about a young Jewish man riding in a bus in the city of New York. A Christian who sat beside him handed him a tract telling about Jesus. After the Jew had read it, the Christian asked him how he felt about Christ.

"I'll tell you what our teacher told us at our synagogue last week," the young Jew replied. "He said he was beginning to think that we Jews have been wrong all these centuries and that Jesus Christ is really the Messiah. For hundreds of years we have heard that He was not God's Son, but now we are beginning to wonder. You look surprised," he added. "So did every Jew there."

He got off the bus then, and the Christian prayed for him

and for Jews everywhere that many would soon come to Christ.

Some day the Jews will all become Christians. That is what Paul says, and now, long after Paul said these things, we are beginning to see a change in the way some Jews feel about Jesus. We should pray much for them.

Here is what Paul says about it.

11:16-36

16 Won't it be a marvelous thing when the whole nation of Israel turns back to God? We know they will because of their holy, God-fearing fathers, like Abraham,* from whom their race has sprung. For the branches of a tree will be the same kind of tree as the roots, and if the original roots of a tree are holy, the branches will be too. 17 But some of the Jews, some of these branches from Abraham's tree, have been broken off.

And you Gentiles, even though you did not come from Abraham, and were branches from, we might say, a wild olive tree, were grafted in, and became part of Abraham's family. So you get the great blessings that God arranged for Abraham and his children, there in God's fat olive tree.

18 But you must be careful not to brag about being put in to replace the branches that were broken off. Remember that you are important only because you are now part of God's tree; you are just a branch, not the root. 19 "Well," perhaps you are saying, "those branches were broken off to make room for us, so we must be pretty good." 20 Watch out! Remember that those branches, the Jews, were broken off because they didn't believe God, and you are there only because you do. Do not be proud; be humble and grateful, and also careful.

21 For if God did not spare those branches that were there in the first place, be careful that something doesn't happen to you too. 22 See how God is both so kind and so severe. He is very hard on those who disobey, but very good to you if you

*Implied.

90

continue to love and trust Him. And if not, you also will be cut off, just as the Jews were.

²³ On the other hand, if the Jews leave their unbelief behind them and come back to God, they will be put back into the tree again with you. For God is able to put them back. ²⁴ For if God was willing to take you, who were far away from God, and make you into branches of His tree, how much more readily will He put the Jews back again who were there in the first place.

²⁵ I want you to know about these things, dear Gentile Christians, so that you will not feel proud and start bragging. It is true that most of the Jews don't understand the gospel now, but this will only last until all of you Gentiles who are going to be saved have come to Christ. ²⁶ And then all Israel will be saved. Do you remember what the prophets said about this? "There shall come out of Zion a Deliverer, and He shall turn the Jews from ungodliness. ²⁷ At that time I will take away their sins just as I promised I would."

²⁸ Right now most of the Jews are enemies of the gospel and they hate it, which has resulted in God's giving His gifts to you Gentiles. But the Jews are still beloved of God, because of the promises to Abraham, Isaac, and Jacob. ²⁹ For God can never go back on His promises. He will certainly do for the Jews all that He said He would.

³⁰ Once you didn't like God either, but this has all changed now because the Jews refused His gifts, and God has been merciful to you instead.

³¹ So, although the Jews do not believe God now, some day they will, and then they will share in the same mercy from God that you have now. ³² For God arranged that all be sinners so that His mighty mercy could be revealed to all.

³³ Oh, what a wonderful God we have! How great is His wisdom and knowledge! How impossible it is to understand His ways! ³⁴ God is too great for man to understand. No one can help Him know what is best to do. ³⁵ His love is so great that no one can even begin to pay enough to get any of it. ³⁶ For everything comes from God alone, and everything is for His glory.

Let us give thanks to Him forever.

SOME QUESTIONS TO ANSWER:

1. Will the Jews always turn away from Jesus? When will they return?
2. Does God always keep His promises? What about His promises to Abraham that He would bless the Jews?
3. If you cannot understand why God does certain things, what should you do about it?

A PRAYER

O God, our Father and the Father of all those who love Your Son Jesus, thank You for Your great promises to Abraham concerning his children, the Jews. We pray for them again today and ask that many of them will begin to think about Jesus and His great love, and believe that He is truly Your Son from heaven who came to take away their sins. Help us to know how to help them. We ask these things in the name of Jesus Christ, our Lord. Amen.

26
Your Gifts to God

"Dr. Benson," a young man said to his pastor, "I want to serve God and I want to give Him my life. Where shall I go to school so that I can learn to be a preacher?"

"Well, first let me ask you a question," Dr. Benson replied. "Do you think God has cut you out to be a preacher? Do you like to stand up and talk to people?"

"Oh, no!" the young man said. "I dread it very much."

"Do you like to sit at a desk and study long hours at a time?"

"No, I like to sell meat in my store."

"Well," said Dr. Benson, "usually we like to do the things God wants us to do. Maybe He wants you to spend your life selling meat."

"But I want God to have my life," the young man said. "I have to be a preacher."

"No," said Dr. Benson wisely, "you have to be what God wants you to be."

Today in his letter, Paul talks about the many kinds of gifts that God has given to His people. What special ability has God given you?

12:1-16

¹ Please, please, dear brothers and sisters, give all of yourselves to God without keeping back anything, so that He can send you to any job He needs you for,* and you will please Him very much. Since He has done so much for you, is this asking too much in return?

² Don't try to copy those who aren't Christians in the way they talk and act and do. But instead, be a new and different person, with a new way of thinking about things. That is the way to find out what God wants you to do. For then it will be easy to know what is good and right and you will find out exactly what God wants.

³ Now I want to say something else that God has told me to tell everyone of you, something very, very important: Don't be proud. Don't think you are great. Instead, think quietly—and God will graciously help you to do this—about how much He has done for you, because you have asked Him to. ⁴ Each of us is good at certain things.* Just as there are many parts to our bodies, so it is with Christ's body. ⁵ We are all parts of it, and it takes every one of us to make it complete. So we belong to each other and each needs all the others.

⁶ God has made each of us able to do certain things best. So be sure to use the gift God has given you to help the church. If God has given you the gift of preaching, then preach as much as you are trusting God. ⁷ If you are best at helping others, be a *good* helper. Teachers should do a *good* job of teaching. ⁸ Those able to encourage others should work hard at that job. If God has gvien you money, help other people with it, without telling everyone about it. If God has put you in charge of something, take care of it and don't quit.

*Implied.

94

And if He has given you the gift of tact and kindness, use it well. Be cheerful, not grouchy because you have to help them. ⁹ Don't just pretend that you like people, but really love them.

Hate what is wrong. Try to do what is good. ¹⁰ Love each other with true brotherly love, and delight to honor each other. ¹¹ Don't be sloppy in your work. Instead, do it enthusiastically in the very best way you can, because you are working for the Lord in whatever you do.

¹² Be glad because of all that the Lord is going to do for you. When trouble comes, be patient, but, of course, keep praying about the problem.

¹³ If other Christians don't have enough to eat or enough clothes, you give them some. And get into the habit of inviting people home for dinner.

¹⁴ If someone tries to hurt you, pray that God will bless him. Don't ever pray that God will hurt him just because he has hurt you.

¹⁵ When people are happy, you be happy too. Enjoy the Lord with them. But if people are sad, you should be sympathetic and share their sorrow.

¹⁶ Work happily together with each other. Don't try to act big. Don't try to get important people to like you but enjoy the company of people who are not important. And don't think that you are wiser than you really are!

SOME QUESTIONS TO ANSWER:

1. What is it that Paul especially wants you to do with your life?
2. How can you give yourself to God?
3. Paul says that each of us Christians has some special ability that will help the whole church. What might yours be?
4. What are some of the different gifts that Paul mentions?
5. What should we do when someone we don't like is thirsty? When he is angry with us?

A PRAYER

Our Father, we are weak and easily led astray. Help us to always keep our minds in heavenly places so that it will be easy for You to tell us what to do. Help us always to ask You for Your help and to trust You to give it to us. Thank You for Your help. In Jesus' name. Amen.

27
A Rule to End All Rules!

I AM SORRY TO SAY that the woman I'm going to tell you about in this story was married to a man she didn't like very much! He wasn't very nice, and I suppose that was why. He was mean to her and was always scolding her. He wrote out a long list of rules for her to memorize and obey.

Well, after awhile the man died and then a few years later this woman married again. But there was a big difference, because she was very much in love with her new husband. They liked the same things, and had a wonderful time together.

One day when the woman was rummaging around in some old trunks, she came across the long list of rules her first husband had made, that were so hard to obey.

"Well," she exclaimed after she had read through the list

again, "what do you think of that? Almost every one of these rules are things I do all the time for my new husband, and I never think anything about them because I want to do them for him."

You see, the woman had forgotten the rules, but she loved her husband, so now she was glad to do these very same things that were so hard to do before.

Today in Paul's letter he gives us a long list of rules and then says not to worry about remembering them! There is only one rule we need to remember, and if we keep it, we will be keeping all the others. That one law is *loving others*. If we love others, then of course we won't hurt them and we will just naturally obey the laws against hurting them. See how simple it is?

12:17—13:14

¹⁷ Don't ever try to get back at someone when he has hurt you. Always be honest and do things in such a way that everyone can see that you aren't trying to cheat. ¹⁸ Don't quarrel with anyone. Be at peace with everyone, just as much as you possibly can.

¹⁹ And again I say, don't try to hurt people just because they have hurt you. If someone is angry with you, just go away. For God has said that He will pay him back if he deserves it. ²⁰ Feed your enemy if he is hungry. If he is thirsty, give him something to drink. When you do that, you will be "heaping coals of fire on his head." In other words, he will feel ashamed of himself for what he has done to you. ²¹ By doing this you will not be overcome by evil, but you will be overcoming evil by doing good.

¹ Obey the government, and other authorities who are above us. For God is the One who has put them there over us. ² So if anyone refuses to obey them, he is really refusing to obey God, and God will punish him.

³ Remember that policemen, for instance, are not there to

scare people who are being good, but to catch those who are bad. So why be afraid of them? Do what is good and they will like you. 4 For the policeman is sent by God to help you. But if you are doing something bad, of course you should be afraid, for the policeman will have you punished. He is sent by God to punish you if you are doing wrong.

5 So you see, you must obey the laws because that is the way to keep from being punished and also because you will be doing what you know is right.

6 You should pay your taxes too; for the policemen and other people who work for the government have to be paid, so that they can keep on doing God's work against whatever is bad.

7 So we should pay everyone whatever he should have. We should gladly pay our taxes and whatever the law says we must pay to get things from another country. We should obey those who are over us and give honor to those whom God has honored.

8 Pay all your debts except the debt of love for others, which you should never finish paying. For if you love others you will be obeying every one of the Ten Commandments all at once. 9 If you love your neighbor as much as you love yourself, then you won't want to do anything to harm or cheat him. You will not try to kill him or steal from him. And you surely won't lie about him or want what is his. 10 No; when you love someone, you will want to keep him from getting hurt, and you won't need laws to tell you not to hurt him; love likes to do what is right and fully satisfies all the other laws. It is the only law you need.

11 Wake up! Time is flying! This is the time to love others and to be kind to them while you still can.* For soon the Lord will come again. His coming is nearer now than it was when we first believed. 12 The night of waiting is almost gone, and it will soon be the Day of His Returning. So we must quit doing wrong things that we are afraid people will find out about and we must spend our time doing things we aren't afraid for people to see.

*Implied.

[13]We must be honest and true. These are things we will never be ashamed of. We must not spend our time in wild parties and drunkenness, or in adultery and lust, or in fighting, or wishing for things that don't belong to us.

[14] But ask the Lord Jesus Christ to help you live as you should, and don't make plans to enjoy bad things.

SOME QUESTIONS TO ANSWER:

1. Do Christians need to have a list of laws to keep? Why not? Then why does Paul give us so many rules in his letter?
2. Who appointed the President of our country?
3. What are taxes? What are "customs" or "duties"? Should Christians pay them?
4. What is the one law that takes in all the others?

A PRAYER

Dear Lord, thank You for the law of love, for we know that if we love You, we will want to do whatever You want us to. Help us to love other people too, so that we will gladly do for them everything You want us to. In Jesus' name. Amen.

28

What If We Don't Agree?

Justus was the name of a boy who lived in the city of Rome long ago. He and his friend Lucius were Christians, and went to the same church, but one day they had a quarrel.

Can you guess what it was about? Well, you see, Justus had to go down to the meat market to get something for dinner, and Lucius went along.

Justus started to go into one of the markets, down in the temple area, where the priests sold the cows and sheep that had been brought as sacrifices to the idols.

"Justus!" Lucius exclaimed. "You wouldn't go in there, would you?"

"Why, sure," said Justus, "why not? It's wonderful meat. The people who bring it to the temple bring only the very best. Go anywhere else, and you're apt to get tough old stuff that you can hardly eat. Come on in and help me pick out a good roast."

"Well, I certainly won't," said Lucius. "It's wrong to buy that meat. As a Christian you should stay a hundred miles away from it, because people will think that you worship idols if they see you in there."

"Don't be silly," Justus said. "We always buy our meat here, and I guess we're as good Christians as you and your family are."

When Justus got home, he told his father about what had happened.

"Well, that settles that," said his father. "From now on, let's get our meat somewhere else, even if it's tougher. It surely isn't worth starting a big quarrel in the church over something like that!"

The next day when Justus told Lucius what his father had said, Lucius felt ashamed of himself. "I'll not buy any meat there myself," he said, "but if you want to, go right ahead, and I won't be angry with you."

Christians today have some disagreements too, just as they did then. Going to good shows or seeing them on television, smoking, drinking coffee, playing cards, playing dominos; all these are examples of things some Christians think are all right and some don't. Often it depends on the part of the country where one is born. Playing dominos, for instance, is considered fine fun by most of us and yet in some parts of the world dominos are a favorite means of gambling and so Christians in such places are brought up to feel that playing dominos is very wicked. And so they never play with them. Today we read Paul's answer to these serious problems.

¹ Give a big welcome to those who want to join you as members of the church, even if they barely believe that Christ alone can save them; but then don't argue in front of them about things the Bible doesn't say are right or wrong.

² For instance, don't argue about whether or not you should eat meat that has been offered to idols. You may think it is all right for a Christian to do this, but one whose faith is weak may think it is wrong, and he will go without any meat at all and just eat vegetables rather than eat that kind.

³ If you are one of those who thinks it is all right to eat that kind of meat, don't go around thinking everyone is silly who believes he should not eat it. And if you are one of those who thinks it is wrong, don't be angry with a Christian who does it. For God has accepted him to be His child. ⁴ He is God's servant, not yours. So you don't need to tell him what to do. He is responsible to God, not to you, and God will help him do what he should.

⁵ And then there is the person who thinks that God wants Christians to keep the Jewish holidays as special days for worshiping God, but others say that it is wrong and foolish to go to all that trouble. Well, everyone must make up his own mind.

⁶ The one who observes special days for worshiping God in special ways does it to honor the Lord, and the one who doesn't is also honoring the Lord, because he is doing what he thinks God wants him to do. And in the same way, the person who eats meat that has been offered to idols gives thanks to the Lord for it, and so he is doing the right thing. And the person who won't eat it is thanking God that he has been saved and is no longer connected with idols.*

⁷⁻⁸ We cannot decide these things just by what we think would be nicest, but we are the Lord's, and we must decide what He wants us to do about them.* We are His while we live; we are still His when we die. So whether we live or die, we are completely the Lord's servants, ready to obey Him, whatever He says. ⁹ That is why Christ died and rose again,

*Implied.

so that He could be our Lord and tell us what to do while we are alive and then afterwards when He takes us home to glory.

¹⁰ So you have no right to try to say a person is bad because he doesn't agree with you about these things. Remember that each of us is going to stand before the Judgment Seat of Christ. ¹¹ For it is written, "As I live, saith the Lord, every knee shall bow to me and every tongue shall confess to God."

¹² Every one of us shall give account of himself to God. ¹³ So, let's not get angry with each other any more about these things. Worry instead about whether you are hurting some Christian brother by encouraging him to sin if he does something he feels is wrong, because you are doing it.

SOME QUESTIONS TO ANSWER:

1. If there is something you think is all right to do, but your Christian friends think it is wrong—should you go ahead and do it anyway?

2. Should you do it if your Christian friends think it is all right, but you think it is wrong?

3. Should you try to stop them from doing it? Should you try to keep them out of the church?

A PRAYER

Father, help us to give up things we like if it will help others to live better lives for You. Help us not to be angry with people who don't agree with us. Help us to grow as Christian brothers and to become of one mind so that we can serve You best of all. In Jesus' name. Amen.

29

It's All Right, But Don't Do It

HERE IS THE STORY of a father who wanted to teach an important lesson to his son. He went out under a tree and gathered up a handful of branches that were small enough to break quite easily. The father tied them together with a piece of string so that they became such a bundle that the boy could hardly hold them in his hands.

"Now," said the father, "I will give you a dollar if you will break these branches in two." The boy tried with all his strength, but couldn't make them bend.

"I can't do it, Dad," the boy said. "Let's see you try."

"It's easy," his father said. "All you have to do is to break them one at a time."

So he untied the string and took each one and broke it easily. And so it is in the church. If we stand together, then Satan doesn't have a chance. But if there is trouble in the church, and we are all apart from each other, then it is easy for him to break us. Trouble in the church is one of the worst things there can be and it hurts God very much. So it is far better to give up something that is all right than to start trouble over it. Here's what Paul says about this:

14:14—15:7

¹⁴ As a matter of fact, I am sure, as a servant of the Lord Jesus, that there is nothing really wrong with eating meat which has been offered to idols. But if someone feels that it is wrong to eat it, then he shouldn't do it.

¹⁵ And it would be most unkind of you to go ahead and eat it if someone else is there who thinks you are doing wrong. Christ died for him, so don't you dare ruin him by what you want to eat. ¹⁶ So even if you think it is all right, but it is going to hurt someone else, don't do it. ¹⁷ Our job as Christians is to help people be good and to have peace and joy in the Holy Spirit, not to eat or drink some particular thing. ¹⁸ And if you do what Christ wants you to about such things, God will be glad, and so will your friends.

¹⁹ So let's try to do and say things that make other people glad and will help them. ²⁰ Don't hurt God's work just for a few chunks of meat. Remember again, that there is nothing wrong with the meat, but it is wrong for someone to eat it when he thinks he shouldn't.

²¹ It is a good thing to quit eating meat and drinking wine or doing anything else, if it is going to bother your Christian brothers or lead them to do things they think are wrong, or things that make them angry or less useful to the Lord.

²² You may know that it is all right to do these things, so far as God is concerned, but keep it to yourself; don't flaunt your faith in front of others who might be hurt by it. For blessed is the man who does not do things that hurt his conscience. ²³ So if a person thinks something is wrong, then he shouldn't do it. He sins when he does it, even if it is all right;

for he thinks that it isn't good, and if he does something he thinks is wrong, then for him it is wrong and he is sinning.

[1] So we who are strong Christians must be careful about the things we do so that we won't worry the weaker Christians. [2] We can't do things we want to do if it will bother our friends.

We have to learn to please and help them, not just to please ourselves. [3] Christ didn't do what He wanted, but what would help others. The prophets said of Him instead of pleasing Himself* that He would come and suffer under God's anger against those who sinned. [4] The Bible tells us this to encourage us and make us happy and patient, even when we can't do some things we would like to.*

[5] So I hope that God, who makes us patient and encourages us, will help you to agree happily with one another just as Jesus wants you to.

[6] And then all of us together can unitedly praise God, who is the Father of our Lord Jesus Christ.

[7] So warmly welcome each other into the church, just as Christ has warmly welcomed you, and God will be glorified.

SOME QUESTIONS TO ANSWER:

1. If you think something is all right, but other people don't, what should you do about it? Give an example.
2. What is one of the best ways for a church to bring glory to God?
3. What should you do if you are angry with another Christian who is doing something you think is wrong, but the Bible doesn't say so?

A PRAYER

O Lord Jesus, who died to make us part of Yourself, help us to love You most of all, and to love each other more and more. Please help us not to get angry with each other when we don't agree. Help us instead to be quiet and thoughtful about others and to try to make them happy. In Jesus' name. Amen.

*Implied.

30
God
Wants
Missionaries

WILLIAM CAREY, the young man who could scarcely make a living by repairing shoes, and had almost no education, was reading a speech. In front of him were many ministers. They did not agree with him. For William Carey was telling them that they ought to send a missionary to India. In fact, they ought to send many missionaries to many parts of the world.

Finally, one of the ministers could stand it no longer. "Sit down, young man," he shouted, "if God wants the heathen converted, He will do it without your help or mine."

You see, the churches in those days, two hundred years ago, didn't think that God wanted His people to go everywhere preaching the gospel. They didn't think that God was talking to them when He said, "Go into all the world, and preach the gospel."

Isn't it wonderful that William Carey finally went anyway? And isn't it wonderful that Paul didn't feel the way those ministers did? For Paul was ready to die if need be, just so he could bring the gospel to us Gentiles. He was God's special messenger to us. And God is still waiting for others to be His messengers. Will you be one of them?

15:8-22

8 Remember that Jesus Christ spent almost all His time with the Jews, because God had promised them a Saviour, and God's promises never fail. 9 But God had mercy on the Gentiles too, so that they might praise God for His mercy to them. That is what the verse in the Old Testament means when it says, "I am going to tell the Gentiles about God and praise Your name among them."

10 And in another place, it says, "Be glad, O you Gentiles, along with His people, the Jews."

11And in still another place, "Praise the Lord, O you Gentiles. Let everyone praise Him." 12 And the prophet Isaiah said, "There will arise one out of King David's family who will be King over the Gentiles, and they will trust Him to be their Saviour."

13 So I pray for you Gentiles, that God who is so kind will keep you happy and full of peace, as you believe in Him. I pray that God will help you to trust Him more and more because He has given you His Holy Spirit to help you do this.

14 I know that you are wise and good, dear brothers, and that you already know these things so well that you are able to teach them to each other. 15 But even so, I wanted to write about them again because I know that all you need is to be reminded by me, for I am God's special messenger to you.

16 God has given me the job of helping and teaching you Gentiles. My job is to help you to offer yourselves to God in the right way, doing what God wants, and being made acceptable by the Holy Spirit. 17 I am so thankful to the Lord Jesus because of the way I have been able to help you become better Christians. 18 For Christ has greatly used my words and

deeds to bring the Gentiles to God. [19] And the Holy Spirit has done great miracles through me. As a result, I have preached the gospel of Christ all the way from Jerusalem clear over to Illyricum.

[20] My idea has been to preach the gospel where the name of Christ is not known, rather than helping where a church has already been started by someone else. [21] For the Bible says that people who have never heard of Christ before must be brought to Him to be saved. [22] That is why it has taken so long for me to come to you.

SOME QUESTIONS TO ANSWER:

1. Who are the Gentiles? Who was the first missionary to them?
2. Did Paul prefer to preach in new territory or where others had already preached? Why?
3. Where did Paul plan to visit next? Why had he waited so long before coming?

A PRAYER

Our Father in heaven, thank You for sending Paul to the Gentiles, so that they too could hear the Word of God and become Your children. And now, our Father, send me wherever You will; help me to do Your will and not my own, even as Paul waited so long to visit his friends in Rome, because You wanted to use him in other places first. Help me to want always, "Not my will, O Lord, but Yours." In Jesus' name. Amen.

31
To Jerusalem with a Gift

A MAKE-BELIEVE STORY is told about three women who were having an argument. Each one thought her hands were the most beautiful. One was sitting by a stream and dipping them gently into the water to keep them pure and white; another was using juicy strawberries to make her fingers a lovely pink color; the third was gathering violets until her hands were lovely with perfume.

An old man passed by. "Who will give me a gift," he asked, "for I am poor?"

None of them would. But another woman standing there, whose hands were not clean, or pink, or fragrant, reached into her purse and gave him a coin.

The old man asked what the three women were arguing about, and they held up their hands for him to see.

"Yes, indeed, they are very beautiful," he said.

"Which do you think is the most beautiful, old man?" the three women asked eagerly.

"Well," he said, "that is another question. I don't think any of them are. It is not the hands that are clean or perfumed with flowers that are the most beautiful. The most beautiful are the hands that give to the poor."

As he said these words, his wrinkles disappeared and he stood before them as a beautiful angel from heaven, whom God had sent to test them, and he gave a crown to the woman who had been willing to help the poor.

Today we learn about some others who will get special awards. Will you be among them? You can, you know. Here's how.

15:23-33

²³ Now at last I am ready to come to visit you. My work is finished here, and you know how much I have wanted to see you all these years. ²⁴ So when I take the trip to Spain that I am planning, I will stop off there in Rome to visit you, and then after we have had a good time together, you can start me on my way again.

²⁵ But first I must go down to Jerusalem to help the Christians there. The special reason for my going there now is to take a gift to the Jerusalem Christians. ²⁶ You see, the Christians in Macedonia and Achaia have taken up an offering for some of the Christians at Jerusalem who aren't getting enough to eat. ²⁷ They were very glad to do this, and feel that they owe this to them, because the news about Christ came to them from the Christians in Jerusalem. And since they received a spiritual gift, the gospel, from those in Jerusalem, they can at least give a gift of some food in return.

²⁸ As soon as I have delivered this money to them and thus finished the job the Christians here have given me to do, then I will come to see you on my way to Spain. ²⁹ And I am sure that when I come the Lord will give me a blessing for you.

[30] There is one thing I want to ask of you. Please, for the Lord Jesus Christ's sake, and because the Holy Spirit gives you love, pray earnestly for me. [31] Pray that I will be protected from those who are not Christians there in Jerusalem. Pray also that the Christians there will be willing to take the money which I am going to bring to them. [32] Then I will be able to come to you with a happy heart by the will of God and we can have a restful time together.

[33] And now, may our God, who gives peace, be with you all. Amen.

SOME QUESTIONS TO ANSWER:

1. Whose hands did the angel say were the most beautiful? Why?
2. What errand did Paul have to do first before coming to Rome?
3. What two things did Paul ask his friends to pray about?

A PRAYER

Our Father in heaven, You have given us everything. Help us to give back to You our time, our money and our prayers. Help us to want to give You more and more, and to keep less and less to spend on ourselves. Help us to take care of those who need our help. In Jesus' name. Amen.

32

Greetings
to
Old
Friends

ONE HOT DAY a family traveling down the highway between Johnstown and Jamestown stopped at Farmer Jones' place to ask for a drink of water, which he gladly gave them.

"Where are you headed?" he asked them.

"We're moving from Johnstown to Jamestown to live," they told him. "Can you tell us what the people there are like?"

"Well, what kind of people did you find where you lived before?" Farmer Jones asked.

"Oh, they were the very worst kind!" the people said. "They were gossipy and unkind and indifferent. We are glad to move away."

"Well, I'm afraid you'll find the same in Jamestown," replied Farmer Jones.

The next day another car stopped, and the same conversation took place. These people were moving to Jamestown too.

"What kind of neighbors will we find there?" they asked.

"Well," said Farmer Jones, "what kind of neighbors did you have where you lived before?"

"Oh, they were the very best! They were so kind and considerate that it almost broke our hearts to have to move away."

"Well, you'll find exactly the same kind again," Farmer Jones replied.

Paul too had many friends. But if he had not been kind and friendly himself, no doubt the story would have been quite different. "He who would have friends must show himself friendly," is an old proverb. As we read Paul's letter today, notice what kind of a person he must have been.

16:1-16

¹ A dear Christian lady named Phoebe, from the town of Cenchrea, will be coming to see you soon. She is a fine worker in the church there. ² Please help her in every way you can and treat her as you would one of our Lord's own friends, for that is what she is. She has helped many when they were in need, and she has helped me very much too.

³ Tell Priscilla and Aquila "hello." They have been of great help to me in my work for Christ Jesus. ⁴ In fact, they risked death for me, at the time it looked like I was going to be killed. I am very thankful to them, and so are all the Gentile churches. ⁵ Also, please give my greetings to the folks that meet for church in their home.

Tell my good friend Epaenetus "hello." I remember him well as the very first person to become a Christian in Asia. ⁶ Remember me to Mary too, who has worked so hard among you. ⁷ Then there are Andronicus and Junias, my relatives, who were in prison with me. They are respected by the apostles, and became Christians before I did. Please give them my greetings.

⁸ Say "hello" to Ampliatus, whom I love as one of God's own children. ⁹ Tell Urbanus, our helper, and Stachys that I love them. ¹⁰ Then there is Apelles, a good man whom the Lord approves of. Greet him for me, please. And also give my best regards to the folks working over at the house of Aristobulus.

¹¹ Remember me to Herodion, my relative. Remember me to the Christian slaves over at the Narcissus' house. ¹² Say "hello" to Tryphaena and Tryphosa, the twins, who are fine workers for the Lord; and to Persis, also a hard worker for the Lord and much loved. ¹³ Greet Rufus for me, who is one the Lord picked out to be His own; and also his dear mother who has been such a mother to me too. ¹⁴ And please give my greetings to Asyncritus, Phlegon, Hermes, Patrobas, Hermas, and the other men who are there with them.

¹⁵ Give my love to Philologus, Julia, Nereus, and his sister, and to Olympas, and all the Christians who are there with them. ¹⁶ Shake hands warmly with each other, as Christian brothers and sisters.

All the churches here send you their greetings.

SOME QUESTIONS TO ANSWER:

1. Friendliness makes people friendly. Do you think the people in Rome would want to be more friendly after receiving Paul's letter?

2. Can you think of someone to whom you could write a friendly letter?

3. Can you think of anyone you have not been friendly to, with whom you can start being friendly? Would this be pleasing to the Lord?

A PRAYER

Lord Jesus, make us friendly. Help us to love other people and to want to help them whenever we can. Help us to have the joy of the Lord in our hearts, and to share it with others. In Jesus' name. Amen.

33

Sincerely Yours, Paul

BETTY AND JIMMY came rushing into the house all excited. "Daddy," said Betty, "come quick! We're rich! We've found a whole bunch of gold down in the river! The sand is full of it!"

"There must be millions and millions of dollars in it, but we're going to give some of it to you and Mother," Jimmy said.

"Well, this sounds interesting," said Father, not becoming too excited. "Suppose we go and see."

"It really is, Dad," said Jimmy and Betty. "It's all over the place! Jimmy and I were just walking along, and we saw something glittering in the sunlight and we ran over there, and there was all this gold."

Soon Jimmy and Betty and their father were looking at the

gold. The children jumped up and down with joy as their father stooped down and picked up a handful of the sand that was full of the little yellow particles. He still didn't look very excited. All of a sudden Jimmy and Betty stopped jumping up and down.

"What's the matter, Daddy," they asked. "Isn't it gold?"

"No," said the father, "I'm sorry to say that it isn't. This is what's called 'fool's gold.' And it has fooled a lot of people in the past. It looks quite a little like gold, but it's something entirely different. It isn't worth anything at all."

Jimmy and Betty learned the hard way that everything that glitters is not gold. And so it is sometimes in the church. The one who preaches the most beautifully may not be preaching for God. The sermon may be full of "fool's gold" that seems wonderful but isn't at all.

It is with this final warning that Paul's letter comes to an end. I hope you realize how wonderful a message it has brought us of salvation for all and of how to grow strong in the Lord, and best of all, remember that this is God's Word, true gold. It is not just a letter from Paul, but it is God who has been talking to us, telling us the wonderful things He wants us to know. And so here are the last words of this life-changing letter; listen to them as though you might never have a chance to hear them again.

16:17-27

[17] And now there is one more thing I want to say to you before I end this letter:

Stay away from people who cause friction and arguments by teaching things about Christ that aren't true. [18] Teachers like that aren't working for our Lord Jesus, but for themselves, trying to get rich. They are good speakers and sound very good when they talk, and simple people are fooled by them.

¹⁹ But everybody knows that you have not been fooled, but stand true and always obey Christ. This makes me happy indeed. When these people try to stir up trouble,* you keep on teaching more and more of what is right, and don't fight, ²⁰ for God, who wants peace, will soon take care of the situation and help you crush Satan under your feet.

Good-bye, and God bless you.

P.S., ²¹ Timothy, my fellow worker and Lucius, and Jason and Sosipater, my relatives, send you their good wishes.

²² I, Tertius, the one who is writing this letter for Paul, send you my greetings too, as a Christian brother.

²³ Gaius says to tell you "hello" for him. I am a guest in his home. The church here meets in his house too, and his home is always open to all.

Erastus, the city treasurer, sends you his greetings, and so does Quartus, a Christian brother.

²⁴ Good-bye again, and may the grace of our Lord Jesus Christ be with you all.

²⁵ I commit you to God who is able to make you strong and steady in the Lord because of all that Christ has done. This is God's great plan for you, a plan that He has kept secret since the world began, until now. ²⁶ But now it is no longer a secret, and as the prophets foretold and as God has commanded, this message is now being made known to all nations so that they will have faith and obey Christ.

²⁷ To God, who alone is wise, be the glory forever, through Jesus Christ, our Lord, Amen.

SOME QUESTIONS TO ANSWER:

1. What does Paul say we should do about people who want to teach us things that are against the Bible?
2. Name some important lessons you have learned from this letter.

*Implied.

A PRAYER

Our Father, keep us from evil, and help us to know how to defeat in a Christlike way those who want to lead us into evil. We thank You for this letter from Paul to the Romans. Help us to remember always the lessons it has taught us. In Jesus' name we ask these things. Amen.

34
"Dear Timothy"

Today we begin to read the first two letters that Paul wrote to his young friend, Timothy. Timothy became a Christian as a result of listening to Paul preach, although he had been brought up in a wonderful home where his mother and grandmother were both Christians. We don't know very much about his father, but perhaps he was not living.

Timothy grew to be a strong Christian very rapidly, even though he was only a young man, much younger than most of the other leaders in the church.

But he was a quiet, timid sort of fellow, not a strong leader. How then could he do his job of rebuking those who were wrong? For rebuking is one of the jobs of a minister, just as teaching is. He needed to learn to be bold.

So one day Paul called together the elders of the church,

and they laid their hands on Timothy's head and prayed, and it was evidently at that time that God gave to Timothy some very special abilities to do God's work.

Paul had gone elsewhere to preach, leaving Timothy to care for the church in Ephesus. Paul wrote back to him, giving him further ideas as to what to do, and also encouraging him and helping him.

I Timothy 1:1-11

¹ Dear Timothy: This is Paul, writing to you; yes, Paul, the missionary, sent out at the commandment of God our Saviour and of Christ Jesus, our hope.

² Timothy, you are just like my own son to me because I was the one who led you to Christ. I am praying for you that God our Father and Christ Jesus our Lord will give you graciousness, a concern for others, and peace of heart.

³ I asked you to stay there in the city of Ephesus while I went over to Macedonia, so that you could prevent people in the church there from teaching things that aren't true. ⁴ For some of those folks there are making up all kinds of wild ideas and talking about being saved through angels instead of by Christ. People are getting all mixed up and confused, instead of growing in faith and in God's grace. ⁵ What I long for them to have is a warm love from a pure heart, a clean mind and a strong faith.

⁶ But some have missed the whole idea of why they are teaching, and instead of teaching these important things, they are arguing and talking foolish nonsense instead. ⁷ They want to become famous as teachers of the laws of Moses when they really haven't the slightest idea what it is all about. ⁸ Of course we should obey the Ten Commandments, but that isn't the way to be saved. ⁹ And remember this, that these laws aren't needed by those whom God has saved, but by sinners, who hate God, so that they can be punished; yes, laws are for those with evil minds, and for people who curse and swear, or who attack their fathers and mothers, and for murderers.

122

¹⁰ These laws are made to punish those who defile women and to punish those men who marry other men, and for slave dealers and liars and for anybody else who does what God says is wrong.

¹¹ And I am God's messenger to tell everyone what the good news of the glory of the blessed God has to say about all these things.

SOME QUESTIONS TO ANSWER:

1. Which three people were especially helpful to Timothy in becoming a Christian?
2. Why did Paul ask Timothy to stay at Ephesus?
3. What were some of the wrong things that the teachers in Ephesus were saying?

A PRAYER

Dear Lord in heaven, thank You for this letter of Paul's to Timothy. As we read it, help us to learn the lessons that will help us to serve You best. In Jesus' name we ask these things. Amen.

35

You Are an Example

ONE NIGHT WHEN HE WAS in St. Louis, Mr. Moody, a famous preacher of many years ago, preached on the text "Believe on the Lord Jesus Christ, and you will be saved." A newspaper published the sermon the next morning with big headlines "How a Jailer Got Caught." A copy of the paper was taken into a jail where a burglar named Burke was awaiting trial for robbery.

"Ha," he said, "that's wonderful. It serves him right." He picked up the paper and began reading it and discovered that he had been fooled and that it was just a sermon. He swore and threw the paper down. But later in the morning he picked it up again and read it all the way through. As a result, he became a Christian.

When his case came up for trial, the officials saw how

changed his life was, and they let him go. He went to New York for awhile, and when he got back to St. Louis the sheriff sent for him and asked him to be a deputy sheriff!

"When you were there in New York," the sheriff told him, "I had you followed by some of my men, and they couldn't find a thing you did that was wrong. Now I see that your change is real and that God has really done something for you."

One of his first jobs as deputy sheriff was to watch over a lot of diamonds in a jewelry store, because the sheriff told him there was no one else he could trust!

Today Paul tells us just a little bit about what he was like, before he became a Christian. He hated Christians then and did his best to hurt them and that is why he felt that he was one of the greatest sinners in all the world, for he was hurting Christ when he hurt the Christians. But even so, God had mercy on him and saved him, and he became a wonderful example of what God can do for people who are converted. He begs Timothy to be an example too, and would say the same to you and me. What kind of an example are you? Do people realize that you belong to Jesus Christ?

1:12-20

12 How thankful I am to Christ Jesus, our Lord, that He has given me the strength to be one of His messengers, and to be faithful to Him, 13 even though I used to hunt down the Christians and call them names and throw them into jail, thus blaspheming the very name of God. But God had mercy on me because I did not realize what I was doing, since I didn't know Christ at that time.

14 Oh, how kind our Lord was, showing me how to trust in the Lord and to become full of Christ Jesus' love!

15 And how true it is, and oh, that everyone would believe

125

it, that Christ Jesus came into the world to save sinners like me—and I was the greatest sinner of them all. [16] But God had mercy on me so that Christ Jesus could use me as an example, to show everyone how patient He is with even the worst sinners, so that others will realize that they too can be saved. [17] Glory and honor be to God forever and ever. He is the King of the ages, the invisible One who never dies; He alone is God, and is full of wisdom. Amen.

[18] Now Timothy, my son, this you must do: fight well in the Lord's battles, just as the Lord has already told us you would. [19] Hold tightly to your faith in Christ, and always keep your conscience clear, doing what you know is right. Some people, as you know, have not obeyed their consciences but have done things they knew perfectly well were wrong, and then, the next thing we knew, their faith in the Lord was gone too. [20] Hymenaeus and Alexander are two men like that, and I had to give them over to Satan to punish them, until they have learned not to bring shame to the name of Christ.

SOME QUESTIONS TO ANSWER:

1. Why did Paul say that he was the worst sinner who ever lived?
2. Why did God let Paul help, after all the bad things he had done? Will God let you help, or just certain ones of His children? What can you do?
3. Why did Christ Jesus come into the world?
4. What is the difference between *being* good and *doing* good? Which pleases God most?

A PRAYER

Our Father in heaven, thank You for the Lord Jesus Christ. Thank You that He came into the world to save us who have sinned so much more than we realize. Thank You for having mercy upon us and giving us eternal life, and for helping us live lives that will please You. In Jesus' name. Amen.

36

A Lesson on Prayer

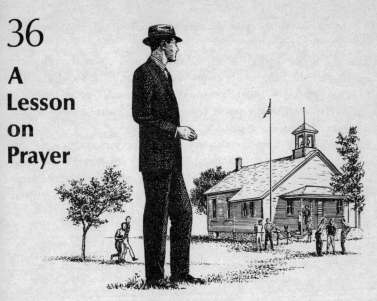

IT WAS A COUNTRY SCHOOL but one of the roughest in the county; and it was the teacher's first job since getting out of college. The man who had taught there the previous year was supposed to be a very good teacher, but the children in this school were so noisy and rowdy that he refused to teach there again. Once the older boys had pushed him out of the room and locked the door behind him. And they were getting ready to do the same thing to the new teacher.

No matter what he did, they refused to cooperate. As days went by, the situation became worse and worse. Finally the teacher gave himself to prayer. He spent a whole night on his knees. As morning dawned, the burden was still there, heavier than ever. But just as the sun was rising, suddenly the prayer was answered, and he knew that all would be well. That morning every step of the way to school (a mile or more) was one of praise.

The boys and girls were all there, but it was as though their natures had absolutely changed overnight. The room that day was perfectly quiet, perfectly orderly, and even more, it marked a turning point from that day forward. There was scarcely any more trouble whatever.

Yes, how God loves to answer our prayers even as He did in this true story! The trouble is that we really don't give Him very much chance to help us, because we don't pray very much. Today Paul gives some instruction on prayer, so let's listen carefully.

2:1-15

¹ First of all, you should learn to pray for others, pleading that God will help them, and giving thanks for what He is going to do.

² Such prayers should be made for kings and all others who are in authority over us so that we can live in peace and quietness, spending our time doing good things and thinking much about the Lord. ³ For this is good and pleases God our Saviour. ⁴ For He longs for all to be saved and to understand ⁵ that God is on one side and all the people on the other side, and Christ Jesus, Himself man, is there between them to bring them happily together.

⁶ He gave Himself to die for everyone, as became clear at God's appointed time. ⁷ And I have been given the job of telling the Gentiles about it, teaching them what is faithful and true concerning Christ. I don't tell them lies as some people are doing.

⁸ So I want men everywhere to pray, with hands held up before God, free from sin, not angry at others nor full of arguing.

⁹⁻¹¹ And the women should be quiet and sober, wearing modest clothing. People should notice Christian women be-

cause they are so kind and good, not because of the way they fix up their hair or because of the jewels they wear or fancy dresses. [12] I never let women teach men or lord it over them. They should sit quietly and accept what they are taught. [13] Why? Because God made Adam first, and afterwards He made Eve. [14] And Adam was not fooled by Satan, but Eve was, and she sinned as a result. [15] But even though Eve sinned (and so God sent pain to women when their children are born) * He will save their souls if they trust the Lord, living quiet, loving, good lives.

SOME QUESTIONS TO ANSWER:

1. Who did Paul say we should pray for?
2. Does God want all men to be saved?
3. Should Christian women be noticeable for their beautiful dresses? If not, for what should they be noticed?
4. Who can bring God and sinners happily together? How?

A PRAYER

Our Father in heaven, we pray now for the President of our country. Guide him in all the great decisions that he must make. Help him to keep our country at peace. Give him a deep reverence and love for God and help him to trust You always. Bless all governors and mayors, all senators and congressmen, all kings and other rulers in other lands. We ask these things in Jesus' name. Amen.

*Implied.

37

The Church and Its Leaders

FREDDY THOUGHT he had never seen such a nice car as the one parked in front of Mr. Olson's house next door. Freddy knew how much it cost too, because Mr. Olson had told him about it. Freddy had $85 in the bank, but Mr. Olson had paid more than $4,000 for his car, which was more money than Freddy thought he would have all the rest of his life.

There was only one trouble about the whole situation. Freddy knew it, and he thought probably Mr. Olson knew it too. The trouble was that Bill, Mr. Olson's oldest boy, wasn't a very good driver. Bill thought he was very good but he really wasn't at all. When Mr. Olson wasn't with him, Bill would step on the gas and make the tires squeal on the pavement, and go around corners as fast as he could, to see how close he could come to tipping the car over without really doing it.

One day Bill did just what Freddy was afraid he would. He was riding along very fast, and not watching very much, and all of a sudden, another car seemed to be in the way, and there was a crash. After awhile an ambulance came and took both Bill and the driver of the other car to the hospital, and Mr. Olson's car didn't look very beautiful anymore. It was warped, smashed and dented, and they had to drag it over to the junkyard and throw it away.

It was a wonderful machine, but it had a terrible driver.

Paul was anxious that Christ's wonderful church, which He had paid so much for, would have good leaders. That is why he tells Timothy in the letter today to be careful about the kind of men he chose to be pastors, elders, deacons and other officers in the church.

And our churches today must have the same kind of good men, if they are going to be useful to God.

3:1-16

¹ A man who wants to be a pastor has a good ambition.

² He must be a good man whose life cannot be spoken against. He should have only one wife, and must be hardworking and thoughtful, orderly, and always doing kind things. He must be glad to have people stop to visit, and must be good at Bible teaching. ³ He mustn't care for wine, mustn't be a troublemaker, and mustn't be greedy for money.

He must be patient, not always starting fights, and not always wishing that he can have all the nice things that other people have.

⁴ He must have a well-behaved family, with children who obey quickly and quietly. ⁵ For if a man can't make his own little family behave, how can he help a whole church behave?

131

[6] The pastor must not be a new Christian, because he might be proud of being chosen so soon, and pride comes before a fall. Remember what happened to Satan when he became proud.

[7] And he must be well spoken of by people outside the church who aren't Christians so that they won't laugh about his being the pastor, for in that way Satan could hurt the testimony of the church.

[8] The deacons or elders must be the same kind of good, steady men as the pastors. They mustn't say one thing to one person and the opposite to someone else. They mustn't love wine, and they mustn't love money. [9] They must be earnestly following Christ, the hidden source of their faith, and must be kind and good.

[10] Before they are asked to be deacons they should be given some other jobs to do in the church to see if they get along all right, and if they do, then they may be chosen as deacons. [11] The deacon must have a wife who is thoughtful and not always talking about other people, and she must be quiet and faithful in everything she does. [12] Deacons should have only one wife, and should have children who obey.

[13] And if they do well as deacons, they will be well rewarded both by the respect from others and also by developing a great confidence and bold trust in the Lord.

[14] I am writing these things to you now, even though I hope to be there with you soon. [15] But if I don't get there, for awhile, you will know from what I have just written what kind of people you should choose as officers in the church of the living God, which contains and holds high the truth God gives us.

SOME QUESTIONS TO ANSWER:

1. Should a man be an officer of a church or a pastor if his children won't mind? Why not?
2. Should a brand-new Christian be an officer in the church? Why not?
3. Why does it make any difference what the deacon's wives are like?

Our Father in heaven, help us to be obedient so that our fathers can be useful to You in Your church. Bless our church, we pray, and bless those who are responsible to help us. Bless our pastor and each of the other officers. Help them to be faithful in their duties to us and to You and to Your people. In Jesus' name. Amen.

38

Paul Talks About Exercise

ALL SUMMER, every morning before breakfast, Gary had practiced sprinting, running and dodging in his backyard, getting ready for the football season. He charged at the bushes, the trees and the clothesline pole, and then just as he was about to crash into them, stepped nimbly around them, as though they were football players on the other team. And now all the hard work was paying off. "One of the best players in several years here at Piedmont High," the coach had told one of his friends.

Gary was a Christian. He wanted to please God in everything he did. One day he got to thinking about something. "Isn't it strange," he said to himself, "how much time I spend getting ready for football games, and how little time I spend getting ready to fight Satan in the game of life? There are going to be lots of problems, and I had better know what to do about them."

Gary knew how to start getting ready, and he began that very day. Every morning when he first got up, he read thoughtfully from his Bible and then got down on his knees beside his bed and prayed about things on his prayer list.

"Bodily exercise is important," Paul tells Timothy in our reading today, "but not as important as spiritual exercise." Gary thought so too, and did something about it.

Have you?

Do you spend time each day reading the Bible and praying?

3:16—4:16

16 Without question, the way to live a godly life is a marvelous secret, that has now been revealed to us; it is Christ who helps us to live as we should.* He came down to earth and became a Man; then the Holy Spirit came on Him, proving that He is God's Son.* He was served by angels in the wilderness,* and He was told about everywhere and many believed Him; and then He went back again to His glory in heaven.

1 But the Holy Spirit has told us very clearly that just before the Lord comes back, some people in the church will start turning away from Christ and listening to evil teachers with devilish ideas. 2 These teachers will tell lies with straight faces and do it so often they won't even worry about it anymore or even think it is wrong.

3 They will say it is wrong to get married and wrong to eat meat, even though God gave these things to well-taught Christians to enjoy and to be thankful for. 4 For everything that God made is good, and we may eat it gladly if we are thankful for it. 5 When we ask God to bless the food, He will, for He has said that it is good.

6 If you explain this to the other men there, you will be

*Implied.

doing your duty as a good pastor who is full of faith and who knows what the Bible teaches.

7 Don't waste time arguing over foolish ideas about what the Bible means, but spend your time and energy in the exercise of being good. 8 Exercise of the body is good, but exercise of being good is even more important. So practice being a better Christian, because that will help you now in this life, and also in the next life. 9 Surely these things are true and that is why we gladly work so hard and suffer shame; 10 our hope is in the living God who has died for all, and especially for those who have accepted His salvation. 11 Teach these things to everyone, and command them to keep practicing obedience to the Lord.*

12 Don't let anyone say to you, "Oh, you're just a boy! I won't listen to you." Be a person they will want to listen to, and will admire because of the way you teach and live and for your love and faith and your clean mind. 13 So while I am away, carefully read the Scriptures to the church, tell them what they mean, and show the people what they should do and what they should believe. 14 Use the gifts and abilities God has given you. Don't forget about that time when the elders of the church laid their hands on your head and prayed for you, and then one of the men gave a message from God, telling what special abilities God was giving to you at that moment.

15 Remember the things I am telling you, and do them; work hard so that everyone can see that you are doing better and better. 16 Keep a close watch on your own conduct and on what you believe. Stay with what is right, and God will bless you and use you to help others.

SOME QUESTIONS TO ANSWER:

1. How do you get spiritual exercise so that you will be ready for life's battles?
2. Can even boys and girls be examples of what Christians should be like? How do they get that way? Are you that way?
3. What was Timothy to do while Paul was away?

*Implied.

136

A PRAYER

Dear Lord Jesus, help us to be such good Christians that we will be examples of all that You want Your children to be like. Help us to live in such a way that people will not think that we are just children and not very useful to God, but may they admire all that You have done in us. Help us to spend our time in ways that will be useful now and that will prepare us for the battles ahead. In Jesus' name. Amen.

39
The Care of Christian Women Whose Husbands Have Died

ELLEN'S MOTHER AND FATHER had been reading a letter from Grandmother. Now they were just sitting there looking sad and worried. "What's the trouble?" Ellen wanted to know.

"Grandmother is sick," Mother said, "and I don't see how she can keep on living there all alone."

"I don't either," Father said. "I think the time has come to invite her to live here with us."

"For keeps?" Ellen asked excitedly.

Her father nodded, "Yes, I think so," he said. "We'll have to crowd up a bit to give her one of the bedrooms, but we can manage it, I'm sure."

And so a few weeks later Grandmother came to live with them.

What to do about taking care of women whose husbands

have died has always been an important problem in the church. Today Paul talks about this and says that a Christian who doesn't care for his own family is worse than a man who has turned away from God. Let's read about it.

5:1-16

[1] Never speak sharply to an older man, but treat him respectfully just as though he were your own father. Talk to the younger men as you would to a much loved brother. [2] Treat the older women as mothers, and girls as you would your sisters, thinking only clean thoughts about them.

[3] The church should take care of women whose husbands have died, if they don't have anyone else to help them. [4] But if they have children or grandchildren or nephews, those are the ones who should take care of them; for kindness should begin at home, and especially in taking care of our parents, and others in our families. This is something that pleases God very much. [5] But the church should take care of widows who are poor and don't have any relatives, if they are looking to God for His help and spending much time in prayer. [6] But if a widow spends her time running around talking about people and sinning, she isn't a real Christian, and the church shouldn't feel that it must help her.*

[7] Give the people of the church this rule, so that the widows will be careful to live as they should.

[8] But anyone who won't take care of his own relatives when they need help, especially those living in his own family, shouldn't be allowed in the church. Such a person is worse than one who says right out that he doesn't believe in God.

[9] A widow who wants to become one of the special church workers should be at least sixty years old, and have been married only once. [10] She must be well thought of by everyone because of the good she has done, such as bringing up other people's children in her home. Has she been kind to strangers, as well as to other Christians? Has she helped those who are sick and hurt? Is she always ready to do kind deeds?

[11] The younger widows should not become members of this

*Implied.

139

special group, because after awhile they would want to get married again, [12] even though they had promised they wouldn't, and so God would have to punish them. [13] And besides, they are likely to be lazy and to go around from house to house, finding out things they shouldn't about other people and telling everybody else all about it. [14] So I think it is better for these younger widows to get married again and have children and take care of their homes so that no one will be able to say anything against them. [15] For some of these younger widows have already turned away from the church and have done things that only Satan would tell them to do.

[16] Let me remind you again that if any Christian has any widows in his own family, he must be sure to take care of them and not leave it to the church to do. Then the church can spend its money to take care of widows who don't have anyone else to help them.

SOME QUESTIONS TO ANSWER:

1. Which is worse, a girl who doesn't love and take care of her mother, or a person who doesn't believe in God?

2. Should the church take care of poor widows if their children are grown up and able to help them?

3. How should older men be treated?

A PRAYER

Our heavenly Father, we pray that we might have deep, strong love for our mothers and fathers as well as brothers and sisters, and that we might always take care of each other. Teach us to love Jesus more, and to be filled with His love. These things we ask in Jesus' name. Amen.

40

How to Treat Your Pastor

MANY YEARS AGO in England there lived a young pastor, only twenty-one years old, whose name was Jeremiah Horrocks. Even at so young an age he had made wonderful discoveries about the stars. But although he loved his work studying the stars, there was something else he felt was more important, and that was to bring God's blessings to the people who met in his little church each Sunday.

One of the things he wanted most to see in his observations of the skies was the planet Venus moving across the sun. This would have helped him in one of his important scientific discoveries. He knew it was going to happen the next week and he was very happy that he was finally going to see it. Then, as he watched his calendar for the big event, he realized it was going to happen on a Sunday. And so, late

Saturday night he put away his telescope and put aside all distracting thoughts, going to church the next morning to preach as usual.

He mentions this in his diary in words which are now written over his gravestone in the Westminster Abbey: "Called aside to greater things which ought not to be neglected for the sake of subordinate pursuits." By these words, he meant simply that preaching to his people was more important than making great scientific discoveries that all the world would honor him for.

Perhaps the Apostle Paul was thinking about people like Jeremiah Horrocks when he said that we may not know for a long time afterward what a godly man our pastor is.

5:17—6:5

17 Pastors who do their work well should be paid generously and should be highly respected, especially those who work hard at both preaching and teaching. 18 For the Bible says that you should not tie up the mouth of an ox while he is working in a cornfield so that he can't eat as he goes along. And in another place it says, "Those who work should be paid."

19 Don't listen to any complaints against the pastor unless there are two or three people who have seen or heard him do whatever he is accused of. 20 If he has really sinned, then he should be rebuked in front of everyone in the church so that no one else will do what he has done. 21 I solemnly command you in the presence of God and the Lord Jesus Christ and the elect angels that you must do what I have just said, whether the man is a special friend of yours or not. All must be treated exactly the same. 22 Never be in a hurry about choosing your pastor or you may notice his sins and then it would be thought that you were approving evil.

And be sure that you yourself stay away from all sin. 23 (By the way, this doesn't mean you should stay entirely away from

142

wine. You ought to take a little sometimes as medicine for your stomach because you are sick so often.) [24] Remember that the sins of some pastors are such that everybody knows about them, and you can do something about it, but in other cases, only the judgment day will reveal the terrible truth about them. [25] In the same way, everyone knows how much good some pastors do, and in cases where these good things are not known now, they will all be revealed some day.

[1] You Christian slaves should work hard for your owners, and you should respect them so that they can never say that Christ's people are poor workers and that Christianity isn't any good. [2] If your owner is a Christian, don't slow down just because he is your brother, but work all the harder because he is a beloved Christian who is getting the good out of your work.

Teach these truths and encourage people to do them. [3] Anyone who says these things aren't so, and won't listen to what I've just said—well, remember that these aren't my ideas, but are the Lord Jesus Christ's words and that is the way people should believe and act. [4] Anyone who says anything different from this is a proud and stupid quibbler over the meaning of words, getting people jealous and angry with each other so that they start calling each other names and thinking or suspecting all sorts of bad things about each other. [5] These wicked arguers with their evil minds don't know how to tell the truth; they are out to make money. Keep away from them.

SOME QUESTIONS TO ANSWER:

1. Should the church save money by paying the pastor as little as possible?
2. Should missionary societies give their missionaries barely enough to live on, so more missionaries can be sent out?
3. What should we do if someone whispers that the pastor has done something wrong?
4. How hard did Paul tell Christian slaves to work? Why? How hard should Christian workmen work today? Why?

A PRAYER

Our Father, thank You for the pastor of our church and the elders who lead us along in the things of God. Help us to honor them in every way and to obey and help them in every way that we can. Bless all true pastors everywhere who are the shepherds over us, for we are Your flock of sheep who need their loving care. In Jesus' name. Amen.

41
The Danger of Money

Two old friends who had not seen each other for many years met on the street one day. After they had talked for awhile, the first one said to the other, "I understand that you are in great danger."

The other man was very much surprised. He couldn't think of any special danger he was in.

"What do you mean?" he asked.

"Well," the first one said, "I have been told that you are getting rich."

Yes, money can do much good but it can also wreck people. Many and many a person has been ruined when he became rich, for people are often willing to do anything for money even though it is something very wrong. And so they sell their souls. The most dangerous thing in the world is not dynamite or atom bombs, but the love of money. Here's what Paul has to say about it:

6:6-21

⁶ Do you want to be rich? You already are if you are happy and good. ⁷ After all, we didn't bring any money with us when we came into the world, and we can't carry away a single penny when we die. ⁸ So we should be well satisfied without money, if we have enough food and clothing. ⁹ But people who long to be rich, soon begin to do all kinds of wrong things to get more money, things that hurt them and make them bad and send them to hell itself. ¹⁰ For the love of money is the first step toward all kinds of evil things, and some people have turned away from God because of their love for it, and pierced themselves through with many sorrows.

¹¹ O Timothy, you are God's man! Run from all these evil things, and work instead at what is right and good, learning to trust God and love others, and to be patient and meek. ¹² Fight on for God. Hold tight to the eternal life which God has given you and which you have told so many people about.

¹³ I command you before God who gives life to all, and before Christ Jesus, who gave a fearless testimony before Pontius Pilate, ¹⁴ that you do exactly what God says to, so that nobody can find any fault with you until our Lord Jesus comes back. ¹⁵ Then when that time comes, everyone will know that God is the blessed and only One who rules over all as King of kings and Lord of lords. ¹⁶ He alone can never die, and lives in such terrible light that no human being can come to Him. No merely human eye has ever seen Him in His glory,* nor ever will. To Him be honor and everlasting power. Amen.

¹⁷ Tell the people who have a lot of money not to think they are great and not to trust in their money, which will soon be gone, but to trust only in the living God who gives us plenty of everything we need to make us happy.

¹⁸ Tell them to use their money to do good. They should

*Implied.

146

be rich in good works, and should give happily to those in need and always be ready to give to other Christians who are having real money trouble. [19] By doing this, they will be sending their money on ahead of them into heaven; and it will give them a chance to really live a true Christian life down here.

[20] O Timothy, don't fail to do the things which God has told you to do! Keep out of foolish arguments with those who think they know so much and really don't. [21] Some of these people have missed the most important thing in life for they don't know God. The grace of God be with you.

Sincerely,
PAUL

SOME QUESTIONS TO ANSWER:

1. How can we get our money deposited in heaven?
2. Why is it dangerous to want money?
3. Briefly tell the story of the widow's mite (Luke 21:1-4).

A PRAYER

Our Father in heaven, thank You for giving us so many good things like food and homes to live in, and healthy bodies. Help us to give all these back to You and not worry about getting rich. Help us to use our money for You. Thank You that You will keep it safely for us until we get to heaven. In Jesus' name. Amen.

42

Good Advice to a Young Friend

Today we begin reading Paul's second letter to his young friend, Timothy. It is a sad letter in some ways because it was written just before Paul was killed for being a Christian. Perhaps it was the last letter that he ever wrote to anyone. It is a letter from an old man in jail for preaching the gospel.

But it is a wonderful letter from a grand old man, a mighty servant of God.

It is written to young Timothy who was frightened and sick and discouraged. Paul, there in jail, is the one who should have been discouraged, but he cheers up Timothy instead. Listen now to what he says.

II Timothy 1:1-18

¹ Dear Timothy,
It's me again, Paul the missionary of Jesus Christ, sent out

by God to tell men and women everywhere about the eternal life He has promised them.

2 Dear son, may God the Father and Christ Jesus our Lord give you His grace, mercy, and peace. 3 How I thank God for you, Timothy! I pray for you every day, and many times during the long nights I beg my God to bless you richly—the God I have always tried to please, just as my father and grandfather tried.

4 How I long to see you again. How happy I would be if I could, for I remember your tears as we left each other.* 5 I remember how much you used to trust the Lord, just as your mother, Eunice, and your grandmother, Lois, do, and I feel sure you still trust Him just as much now as you used to.

6 Now, Timothy, let me give you a suggestion.** You are too timid and afraid of people.** But you shouldn't be, because when I laid my hands on your head and blessed you, God gave you a special gift of being bold.* Now stir up that gift so that it will be at work inside you and make you strong. 7 For the Lord does not want you to be afraid of people, but to be wise and strong and to love people and enjoy being with them. 8 Then you will never need to be afraid to tell people about our Lord, and you won't be afraid to let people know you are my friend, even though I am in jail for Christ's sake. Instead, be ready to suffer with me for the Lord.

God will help you, 9 for He has saved you and chosen you for His great work, not because you were so good, but just because, long before the world began, He decided to do all this for you through Christ. 10 And now He has done what He promised, for our Saviour Jesus Christ came and saved us from death and gave us everlasting life through trusting Him.

11 And I have the wonderful job of telling everyone this good news. God made me a missionary to the world to teach everyone these good things. 12 That is why I am suffering here in jail, and I am certainly not ashamed of it, for I know the One in whom I trust, and I am sure that He is able to safely guard all I have given to Him until I get to heaven.

*Implied.
**Suggested by context.

[13] Always keep in mind the good things I have taught you, that you used to listen to with so much love and faith in Jesus. [14] And guard well the wonderful truth that God has given you. The Holy Spirit within you will help you keep it safely.

[15] As you know, all the Christians who came here from your part of Asia have deserted me; even Phygellus and Hermogenes are gone.

[16] But may the Lord bless Onesiphorus and all his house, because he visited me so often and helped me and hasn't been ashamed of me because I am in jail. [17] In fact, when he came to Rome, he searched everywhere, trying to find me, and he finally did. [18] May the Lord give him a special blessing at the judgment day. And you know better than I do how much he helped the folks there at Ephesus.

SOME QUESTIONS TO ANSWER:

1. Where was Paul when he wrote this letter?
2. What happened to Timothy when Paul laid his hands on his head?
3. Why had all the Christians there deserted Paul?
4. What was the name of the man who hadn't deserted him?

A PRAYER

Dear heavenly Father, thank You for Paul. Thank You for saving him and leading him along so wonderfully through his life. Thank You that he was so patient in suffering there in jail. Help us to learn to be patient too, and to trust You at all times, no matter what happens to us, knowing that it is for our good. Help us to love You more and more. In Jesus' name. Amen.

43
Getting Hurt Is Good for Us!

ONE SUNNY AFTERNOON in Switzerland, a man went walking up into the mountains, and passed by a little cottage where a shepherd was feeding some of his sheep. One of the sheep was sick, lying on a pile of straw. The man saw that its leg was broken, and he felt very sorry for it.

"How did it happen?" he asked the shepherd.

To his great surprise, the shepherd said, "Sir, I broke that sheep's leg." And then, seeing the look of horror on his visitor's face, the shepherd explained, "Of all the sheep in my flock, this one was the worst. It would never listen to me or do what I said. It never followed along where I was leading the other sheep. It would wander over to the cliffs and many a time was in great danger of slipping off and

151

plunging into the depths far below. And not only was it disobedient, but it was leading the other sheep along with it. I have had other sheep like that, and so I knew what to do. I broke its leg and then bound it up again to heal. The first day afterward when I went to it with food, it tried to bite me. So I let it alone for awhile, and then went back. Now it takes the food and licks my hand and shows every sign of obedience and love. When this sheep is well, as it will be soon, it will be the best sheep of all my flock. No sheep will hear my voice so quickly. None will follow so closely at my side."

Paul had suffered much for the sake of Jesus. He had often been beaten with rods and thrown into jail. Two different times he was shipwrecked on his missionary trips and spent long nights in cold, dangerous waters, not knowing whether he would ever see land again.

But Paul said that he was glad about it all. None had been as far away from the Lord as he, but he had learned through these experiences more and more of God's gentleness, kindness and everlasting love. Paul had come to follow his Lord very closely as a result.

2:1-14

¹ O Timothy, my boy, be strong, with the strength that Christ Jesus wants to give you. ² You must teach others the things you have heard me speak about so often. Teach them to trustworthy men who will pass them on to others also.

³ Take your share of suffering the same as I do, as a good soldier of Jesus Christ. ⁴ And as Christ's soldier, you must not let yourself get all tied up with worldly affairs, or you won't be much good as a soldier. ⁵ And you must follow the Lord's rules in doing His work, just as an athlete does in a game, or else you will be disqualified and get no prize. ⁶ And you must work hard like a farmer who gets paid well if he raises a big

crop. [7] I hope that you can understand what I am trying to tell you; the Lord will help you understand.

[8] Don't ever forget the wonderful fact that Jesus Christ was a Man, born into King David's family; and that He was God,* for He was made alive again after He had been killed. [9] It is because I have preached these great truths that I am in trouble here and have been put in jail as a criminal. But the Word of God is not in chains, even though I am.

[10] I am very willing to suffer so that salvation will go to everyone God has chosen for eternal glory in Christ Jesus. [11] And anyway, when we suffer and die for Christ it just means that we will start living with Him in heaven. [12] If we endure hardships for Him down here, well, remember that we are going to sit with Him in heaven and rule with Him some day. But if, when we suffer, we give up and turn against Christ, then He must turn against us.

[13] But even when we don't have as much faith as we should, He remains faithful and will help us anyway, for He can never lie, and He will do everything for us that He has promised to do. [14] Remind people about these things, and command them in the name of the Lord not to argue about things that aren't important, because that only causes confusion.

SOME QUESTIONS TO ANSWER:

1. Can a fast runner who doesn't obey the rules, win the race? What race are we Christians running? What are some of the rules? What is the goal where we are headed?

2. If you work hard for God but don't obey His rules, will God give you a reward?

3. Why does God sometimes let us suffer?

A PRAYER

Lord, help us to be strong with the strength that Christ Jesus gladly gives us if we ask Him. Help us to be able to get hurt without feeling that You have deserted us, knowing that it is good for us

*Implied.

to suffer and it can help us love You more. Bless those who are
suffering now, and may they find the peace of God. We ask these
things in Jesus' name. Amen.

44
If You Love to Argue

BILL AND FRANK were having a strange argument. They were trying to decide whether Frank should read his Bible.

"You ought to read your Bible more so you can be a good guy like me," Bill said.

"Oh, yeah?" Frank replied hotly. "I don't think you're such big stuff."

"I am too," said Bill. "My mother and Sunday school teacher say I am a fine boy. And I guess they ought to know."

"Ha!" said Frank. "They ought to ask me. I'd tell them a few things. I think I'll quit reading the Bible because you brag around so much."

I'm glad to say that Frank didn't, but it wasn't because of Bill and his bragging. The Bible says the way to help people is by being good and kind, not by arguing with them. I hope that Bill has learned this by now!

How God hates arguments among His people! He wants them to agree and to be happy and to love one another. Paul tells Timothy he shouldn't even talk about the silly ideas some people want to argue with him about. It won't help them, Paul says, and it might hurt them a lot.

What about you? Do you always want the last word like I do? Then let's read together and ask God to help us.

2:15-26

15 Work hard so God can say to you, "Well done." Be a good workman who doesn't need to be ashamed when God examines your work. Know what the Bible says and means.

16 Keep away from silly, foolish arguments. They only make people sin by getting angry with each other. 17 And things will be said that will burn and hurt for a long time to come. Hymenaeus and Philetus are men like that, who love to argue.

18 They have gone astray, preaching that Christ has already come back and that the resurrection of the Christians is already over; and they have wrecked the faith of some who believe them.

19 But God's truth stands like a great rock and nothing can shake it. And these words are written on it: The Lord knows those who are really His; and if a person says he belongs to God, he should be leaving evil things alone. 20 In a rich home there are dishes made of gold and silver, and some made from wood and clay. The expensive dishes are used for guests, and the cheap ones are used in the kitchen, or to put garbage into. 21 Remember that if you stay away from sin, you will be like a dish made of purest gold, the very best in the house that Christ Himself can use.

22 So run from anything that gives you wrong thoughts. Get away fast! Run! But stay close to anything that makes you want to do right. Have faith and love, and be at peace with all those who love the Lord. 23 Again I say, stay away

from foolish questions about the Bible. They only get people angry and upset. ²⁴ And God's people mustn't be in arguments, but they must be gentle, patient teachers of those who are wrong.

²⁵ Don't act big when you are trying to teach mixed-up people what is right. If you talk to them quietly, God is likely to help them turn away from their wrong ideas and believe what is true. ²⁶ Then they will escape from the trap Satan has set for them, for he can catch them easily, any time he wants to, while they are away from God.

SOME QUESTIONS TO ANSWER:

1. What should you do if someone starts to tell you something he shouldn't?
2. Does arguing help a person find Christ? What does?
3. If you become a missionary some day, do you think you should argue with people in other countries about their religion, or should you tell them about Christ?

A PRAYER

Our Father, help us to live clean lives so that You can use us to help others. Help us to spend our time living for You instead of arguing for You. Help us to be gentle and patient with each other so that we can show everyone the power of Christ in our lives. Forgive us for the times we have sinned against You by quarreling. In Jesus' name. Amen.

45

Danger Right Inside the Church

DID YOU EVER HEAR about the robbery in a church? A bandit with a black mask over his face and a gun in his hand walked up to the platform while the minister was preaching and asked him if he would please sit down. Then he courteously told the ushers to come forward with the collection baskets and asked all the people to put in all their money. After this had been done, he put the money in a bag and he walked out and disappeared.

But it doesn't take a masked bandit to rob people who come to church. Sometimes even ministers have robbed people, not of their money, but of their faith in God and their confidence in the Bible. They tell the people that Christ didn't really die for them and that the Bible isn't God's Word. Such ministers are far more dangerous than masked robbers, be-

cause they rob people of their heavenly home. Paul tells
Timothy to beware of such men and to stay away from them.

3:1-13

¹ You might as well know now, Timothy, that in the last
days it is going to be mighty rough to be a Christian. ² People
are going to fall in love with themselves because they will
think themselves so wonderful. They will love money, brag,
sneer, speak evil of others, be disobedient to their parents, be
ungrateful and thoroughly bad.

³ They will be hardhearted, will never give in to others,
will lie, and be full of evil thoughts toward women. They will
be rough and cruel and sneer at people who try to be good.

⁴ They will betray their friends, be hotheaded, soggy with
pride, and love good times rather than loving God. ⁵ They
will go to church, all right, but they won't really believe anything. Keep far away from people like that. ⁶ They are the
kind that craftily sneak into other people's homes and make
friendships with silly, sin-burdened women and teach them
their new ideas. ⁷ Women of that kind are forever following
new teachers, but they never understand the truth. ⁸ And .
their teachers fight truth just as Jannes and Jambres fought
against Moses. They have evil minds, warped and twisted,
and have turned against the Christian faith.

⁹ But they won't get away with all this forever. Some day
everyone will see how wrong they are, just as happened to
Jannes and Jambres.

¹⁰ But you know that I am not that kind of a person. You
know what I believe and the way I live and what I want.
You know my faith in Christ and how I have suffered. You
know my love for you and my patience. ¹¹ You know how
many troubles I have had because of the gospel. You know
all that they did to me when I was visiting the cities of Anti-
och, Iconium and Lystra, but the Lord delivered me.

¹² Yes, and all who decide to live godly lives as Christ Jesus
wants them to will suffer at the hands of those who hate the
Lord Jesus. ¹³ In fact, evil men and false teachers will be-

come worse and worse, fooling people, and themselves being fooled by Satan.

SOME QUESTIONS TO ANSWER:

1. What is a bank robber? What would a faith robber be? What does he do? How does he do it?
2. Which is more dangerous—a bad idea that is put into some-one's head, or a bullet?
3. Should we be friends with people who say they are Christians, but laugh at God's Word?

A PRAYER

O God, our heavenly Father, help us never to become like the men Paul was writing to Timothy about. Help us to live pure, good lives that will bring glory to Your holy name. Help us to be like Paul, who suffered so much for You, and whom You loved so much. We ask these things in Jesus' name. Amen.

46
The Importance of Bible Study

THERE WAS A MAN who read his Bible every day until once someone told him he should listen for God to tell him what to do.

After that he would sit and listen and think about what God would want to tell him instead of reading his Bible to find out.

And then pretty soon he began doing whatever he thought God was telling him to do, instead of what the Bible said to do.

After awhile, though this is hard to believe, he thought that since he needed some money it would be God's will for him to steal some.

You see, this man was deciding by his feelings and wishes rather than by the Word of God. And that is how he got into such trouble.

Paul keeps saying again and again, and he says it again in his letter today, that a young Christian *must* live a good life and know his Bible. Study it, learn it, preach it, and live by it.

A Christian who doesn't know his Bible is in great danger. He can easily be fooled into believing and doing things that are not God's will. That is why Paul says it over and over again.

So what about you? Are you taking time out from your busy hours before school or afterwards, or in the evenings, to read your Bible? If you haven't been doing it, would you start today?

3:14—4:6

¹⁴ Keep right on believing the things you have been taught. You know they are true, for you know you can trust those of us who taught them to you. ¹⁵ You know how, when you were a small child, you were taught the Holy Scriptures, and it is these that make us wise to accept God's salvation by trusting in Christ Jesus.

¹⁶ The whole Bible was given to us by God and is useful to teach us what is true and to make us realize what is wrong with our lives; it straightens us out and helps us do what is right. ¹⁷ It is God's way of making us perfect in every point, and able to do good to everyone.

¹ And so I solemnly say to you before God and before Christ Jesus, who will some day judge the living and the dead when He appears to set up His kingdom, ² preach the Word of God at all times, whenever you get the chance. Scold your people when they need it and encourage them, all the time feeding them patiently with God's Word.

³ For there is going to come a time when people won't listen to the truth, but will go around looking for teachers who will tell them just whatever they want to hear. ⁴ They won't listen to what the Bible says, but will gladly follow their own crazy notions.

⁵ You must stay awake to watch out for all these dangers. Don't be afraid to suffer for the Lord; bring others to Christ, leaving nothing undone that you ought to do.

⁶ I say this because I won't be around to help you very much longer. My time has almost run out. Very soon now I will be on my way to heaven.

SOME QUESTIONS TO ANSWER:

1. Who were Timothy's teachers? Can you name three of them?
2. When is the best time for you to read your Bible?
3. If someone tells you something different than you have been taught, how can you find out whether it is true or not? Do those who teach lies usually use Bible verses to "prove" what they teach? How can this be?

A PRAYER

Our Father, help us to learn the Holy Scriptures, that are able to make us wise and useful to You. Help us not only to read and pray, but to do good, even as You have told us we must. And help us to get the Word of God to others all around the world, so that they also can know what You want them to do and so that they can be saved. In Jesus' name. Amen.

47
A Last Good-Bye

BENNY LOCKE was a train locomotive engineer who had
worked for the Lackawanna Railroad for fifty-seven years.
One day his train was twenty-five minutes late as he started
slowly up the Pocono Mountains.

"I couldn't gain a second on the way up," he said afterwards, "but after we dipped over the top, things began to
break just right for me. It was a beautiful day, with the air
perfectly clear, and we almost flew down the mountain. I
just held her steady and let her go. At last the old station
where we were going loomed up ahead, and as we pulled in
I looked at my watch, and we were just on the dot. As I stood
wiping the sweat from my face, there was a tap of a cane on
the outside of my engine, and on looking out, I saw the presi-

dent of the railroad all smiles, and he said to me, 'A good run, sir; a very good run.'

"That meant more to me than anything that could have happened in this world. And, brother when I make my last run and pull into the Great Terminal up there in heaven, if I can just hear Jesus say, 'A good run, sir; a very good run,' the trials and the struggles down here won't matter."

That is the way Paul felt as he came to the end of his letter to Timothy. Soon after he laid down his pen, he was killed for his preaching.

Now, as he sits there writing the last lines, we can see that he is an old man who has used up his life for God. No doubt he is sitting in a dark, damp dungeon and soon, with winter coming on, it will be very cold, so he needs his coat. But most of all he needs some friends, for most of the Christians there in Rome have turned away from him and he is left to die alone. But the Lord is with him, and that is always enough.

Do you know anyone who is old and lonely, and whom you can befriend?

4:7-22

7 I have fought long and hard for my Lord, and through it all I have kept true to Him. And now the time has come for me to stop fighting and to rest. 8 Up there in heaven a crown is waiting for me which the Lord, the righteous Judge, will give me at the judgment day. And not only to me; there will be crowns for everyone who loves to think about that coming day when we will all see Jesus.

9 Please come as soon as you can, 10 for Demas has left me. He loved the good things of this life, and went to Thessalonica. Crescens has gone to Galatia, and Titus to Dalmatia. 11 Only Luke is with me. Bring Mark with you when you come, for I need him. 12 Tychicus is gone too, for I sent him to Ephesus.

¹³ When you come, be sure to bring the coat that I left at Troas with Brother Carpus, and also the books; and especially the parchments.

¹⁴ Alexander, the coppersmith, has done me a lot of harm. The Lord will punish him, ¹⁵ but you be careful of him, for he fought against everything we said.

¹⁶ The first time I was brought before the judge, no one was here to help me, for all had run away. I hope that the Lord will not blame them for it. ¹⁷ But the Lord was standing beside me and helping me so that I could boldly preach a whole sermon for all the world to hear. And the Lord saved me and I was not thrown to the lions. ¹⁸ Yes, the Lord will always deliver me from all evil and will save me for His heavenly kingdom. To God be the glory forever and ever. Amen.

¹⁹ Please say "hello" for me to Prisca and Aquila, and to those living at the home of Onesiphorus. ²⁰ Erastus stayed at Corinth, but I left Trophimus sick at Miletum.

²¹ Do try to get here before winter. Eubulus sends you greetings, and so do Pudens, Linus, Claudia, and all the brothers.

²² May the Lord Jesus Christ be with your spirit.

Good-bye for now.
PAUL

SOME QUESTIONS TO ANSWER:

1. Why did Paul need his coat?
2. Who was with Paul during his trial?
3. Who will always be with you if you will trust Him?
4. Paul had fought a good fight and finished up his work. What was waiting for him in heaven?
5. What is waiting for you?

A PRAYER

God of our fathers, how can we ever thank You enough for all the good things You have done? We do thank You for Your wonderful plan of rewarding us in heaven for what we do for You down here. Thank You that we will see the Apostle Paul some day and Timothy, and most of all, the Lord Jesus Himself. For all these things we give thanks in Jesus' name. Amen.

Moody Press, a ministry of the Moody Bible Institute, is designed for education, evangelization and edification. If we may assist you in knowing more about Christ and the Christian life, please write us without obligation to: Moody Press, c/o MLM, Chicago, Illinois 60610.